Food for Thought

Celebrating the joy of eating
well and living better

Contents

Food for Thought – an introduction

In 1972 my Mum introduced me to the world of organic farming and soil with a subscription to the Soil Association. It was this beginning that shaped my life's work in food, farming and community. In 2017 I decided to write my story. It flowed easily as a linear stream of consciousness about my life combined with philosophical musings on how we are playing out our lives on Mother Earth.

This book has grown out of that story. It is an offering attempting to look at some of the key pillars for building a just world with its core firmly rooted in food and farming.

It is clear we are facing the biggest challenge in the history of our species and the way we nourish ourselves is central to the solution. We will undoubtedly make better choices by taking a holistic approach to designing a food system from the soil up, not the plate down.

In a matter of just 60 or so years, the Western diet has developed from a relatively stable relationship with food to one of exploitation and indulgence. As Michael Pollan said in an interview with Onnesha Roychoudhuri for Alternet.org in 2008 'We are amazing to be able to design the only diet that makes people sick'. (michaelpollan.com/interviews/michael-pollan-debunks-food-myths)

The world's food industry is more powerful than ever, having vast investments locked into a failed system whose shareholders are reliant on continued exploitation to secure their inflated returns. Our political system allows governments to be lobbied by these powerful forces, meaning positive change is rare and hard won.

It's now up to us the global citizens, to make change through action. There are many encouraging signs that a worldwide wake up is taking place. Grassroots projects and businesses are making it their mission to make a difference both great and small towards a more sustainable food system with equality and justice for all at its core.

My life's work has been passionately devoted to the world of food justice through living community, city farming, community farming and business. I have been privileged to have a business vehicle with which to make a difference. For well over 25 years my company, Better Food, has been championing organic food from local producers and building strong food communities. Retailing food with the wellbeing of the whole community in mind is much needed in a supermarket dominated world.

Better Food's work for the future is to do what we do even better - to overtly celebrate local foods and to continue to make it apparent that this is what we stand for. We will keep telling stories about our wonderful farmers and suppliers, guiding people towards relating to food in a more sustainable way - a way that makes us all feel better and increases our sense of security in a changing world.

We need a food system designed from the soil up, not the plate down

How to use this book

You can dive in and read the whole book back to front if you choose, or feel free to dip in and out if you find yourself drawn to certain chapters. Each chapter delves into the subject using stories from my life to illustrate the ways I think we can do better and offering ideas for making a difference in how we relate to food, farming and community.

The recipes
The 50 or so recipes in this book have no particular theme, rather they accompany the storylines and illustrate my approach to cooking and eating. They are eclectic, practical and one or two may challenge your assumptions about food. There are a dozen or more offered as further gifts by the brilliant contributors to the book, for which I say thank you kindly to them.

RECIPE Look out for recipes

The resources
This book does not attempt to go deeply or scientifically into its subject matter. Its aim is to tell some food stories and to inspire further action for change. My hope is that the resource pages at the end of each chapter will allow you to pursue more deeply any topics that have sparked your interest. Before going to press all of the web resources were present and accessible but due to the nature of the internet of course we cannot guarantee this will be the case at the time you are reading the book.

Ⓡ Look out for the resources symbol

My thanks

My greatest and most loving thanks go to my wife Gerry. It has been her support and patience over 30 or more years that has helped me get on and take action. She has often in the past been the breadwinner, while my uncompromising ideology created debt rather than surplus. Her trust in me to pursue my vision even when it looked like madness with regard to the security of the family is something I am so grateful for. We made it darling!

After I wrote my story it became clear that it was unpublishable as it was. Sue Richardson has worked with me over many months to shape the book and tease out a real purpose for it. Without Sue, I doubt this book would ever have found its voice. Thank you, Sue.

Hugh Fearnley-Whittingstall is a household name as both environmental campaigner and chef and shares many of my views on how we might live for a better world. I was so delighted when he generously agreed to write the foreword for this book. I am unashamedly grateful for the fact that Hugh's name on the cover of my book will naturally encourage more people to pick it up. Thank you, Hugh.

I give thanks to our beautiful earth for feeding us

This book has been enriched by 12 contributors who have offered their perspective on the key pillars of the book. They have added both some mentoring wisdom and pioneering inspiration to my own story, providing diversity and balance to the book for which I am hugely grateful.

Thank you to all the contributors

Ped Asgarian, Julie Brown, Mya-Rose Craig, Meg Doherty, Hugh Fearnley-Whittingstall, Jackie and Alan Gear, Jamie Hartzell, Barny Haughton, Charlie Haughton, Rosemary Haughton, Caroline Lucas, Nathalie Moukarzel, Fiona Provan, Nancy Schwoyer, Jon Young, Liz Haughton for recipes, Lou Marchioni for a recipe.

Foreword by Hugh Fearnley-Whittingstall

When I first walked into Better Food on Whiteladies Road in Bristol I felt a level of excitement about shopping for food that I hadn't experienced in years. It was early autumn and on the pavement outside the shop a stunning display of colourful squashes (including my favourite, the crown prince, with its dusky grey-green skin concealing sunset-orange flesh) vied for my attention alongside wooden crates of beautiful British apples and pears. The organic fruit and vegetables inside were equally bursting with vibrancy and life. They looked as if they'd been picked that very morning, and no doubt many of them had.

As I ventured further inside, taking in the deli counter and the dairy, the dry store shelves (and let's not forget the chocolate and coffee, and of course the booze...) I thought how lucky I was to have just moved within walking distance of this haven of seasonal goodness and rich flavours. And I thought how great it would be if everyone had such a place at the heart of their community.

I could sense this wonderful shop was the vision of somebody who understood that the food we eat, where it comes from and how it is produced, is absolutely central to the quality of our lives. I didn't know at the time that that person was Phil Haughton, the brother of my chef friend Barny, with whom I had collaborated at various food festivals down the years. Nor did I know about the fascinating background to the Better Food story, about Phil's formative childhood encounters, and the youthful passions that made him so determined to find a better way of feeding our bodies and souls.

In fact, even after knowing Phil for several years, and enjoying some rousing conversations about food provenance and food politics (often fuelled by the kind of food and drink that we both get so excited about) I still knew very little about his origins, personal and professional - until the almost complete manuscript of this book landed with an earthy thud in the inbox of my laptop. And here it is. A book of surprising stories and inspiring characters and companions that somehow makes perfect sense of this man and the remarkable business he has built.

There can't be many people whose parents bought them a subscription to the Soil Association as a 14th birthday present. And if only more kids – all kids – had a chance to camp out in wild places, gutting fish in a mountain stream and cooking them over a camp fire; and to harvest fruit and vegetables from orchards and fields, rather than just from the supermarket shelves.

Colourful squash display outside Better Food

> **Food is at the very heart of making the world a better place**

Phil made these vital connections - between the food that nurtures us and a wild, biodiverse countryside that also has the power to nourish and sustain - in his formative years. And somewhere along the way, he resolved to capture and communicate these vital insights in his life's work. Mostly he does this by offering us the best ingredients, curated by his hard-won knowledge of the food system and deeply held belief that it can be better for all of us.

And now, in this book, with his customary generosity and frankness, he sets out the stories behind his insights, and the thinking behind his approach to food. Better sustenance for everybody is vital, of course, but Phil explains that better food is about more than that. It's about shared values and shared stories, of how the best food is rooted in the living landscape, and nurtured by families and communities down the generations.

Never one to hog the limelight, however, he has corralled a diverse and inspiring group of fellow-travellers, and invited them to join the conversation. People like Caroline Lucas, the UK's only Green MP (we need more!) and Mya-Rose Craig, the young naturalist inspiring the next generation. They are right to insist, like Phil, that all is not lost, and that there is still time to find, and insist on, a better way of doing things.

As we face up to an unprecedented set of challenges, both to our health and to the planet on which we all depend for nourishment and resilience, that's more important than ever. Phil knows, and we all need to know, that food, and how we produce it, is at the very heart of making the world a better place.

Kohlrabi salad with lentils and kimchi

I love simple assemblies of seasonal veg with a few punchy 'sprinkles' to add zest. Here the thin but crunchy kohlrabi contrasts with the nutty, yielding lentils, and the kimchi gives a kick. You could easily swap in celeriac, cannellini beans and capers; or carrots, chick peas and harissa... You get the idea!

Serves 2 as a starter

Ingredients

100 g puy lentils
1 medium head of kohlrabi or 2 small ones
About 2 tablespoons of live kimchi
A handful of raisins
A few mint leaves, chopped
A trickle of olive oil
A squeeze of lemon
Salt and pepper

Method

Rinse the lentils well and put in a pan of unsalted cold water. Bring to a simmer and cook for 12–15 minutes until tender but still with a bit of bite. Drain well. Season with a little salt and pepper and dress with olive oil and lemon juice while still warm. Leave to cool.

Peel the kohlrabi and slice very thinly. Arrange over a serving dish.

Mix the lentils with the kimchi and raisins, and spoon on top of the kohlrabi (leaving the edges so you can see the slices).

Finish with another trickle of olive oil, a squeeze of lemon juice and a sprinkle of chopped mint.

Better nature

Building new ways together to mend our broken world

Nature is self-balancing, always in harmony and filled with pure joy. We all subliminally know the power of nature. It is our deep and very old connection with Earth. Not being separate from nature but being an actual living breathing part of it has been in our DNA since before we recognised ourselves as human beings. It is hardly surprising therefore that we seek out nature for walks, for sun, for water. We lean in to listen to the sounds of nature to help us connect to our vital being. The less we pay attention to this foundation of what it is to be human the less we are able to function as balanced people with a sense of inner harmony. The less our children access nature and feel their own wildness, the less connected they are to the nourishing and health-giving wonders of our planet. As children grow up, nature will guide them to make sense of all that is facing us as a human race. Now is a time like no other to build new ways together to mend our broken world. We have detached ourselves from living with our planet to living off it in an increasingly exploitative and disconnected way. We are driving our planet's very balance out of kilter and impacting enormously on wildlife, biodiversity and weather patterns. Humankind is not benefiting from this exploitation. In fact we have unwittingly set about to dehumanise ourselves more and more... as if this is the answer to life.

As XR and Greta are telling us, we need to wake up...

Phil talked to...
Jon Young

Jon Young is the author of several works in the field of deep nature connection mentoring. He worked for 14 years with a group of experienced leaders in nature mentoring to produce and co-author Coyote's *Guide to Connecting to Nature*. He is the founder of 8 Shields, which works to rebuild nature connected communities worldwide. ⓡ

Phil: Tell me, what's important to you about nature?

Jon: Nature returns us to our North Star. It gives us the vision that leads us back to our ancient sensibility. When I say sensibility I literally mean sense-ability. We need to awaken to the longings of our autonomic nervous system and feed into those longings the inputs our bodies, our nervous systems and our very souls really require in order for us to fully flower into the best versions of ourselves.

Over the past 40 years I have had the opportunity to facilitate exactly this with thousands of people and seen the most amazing changes occur. Connecting with nature helps people become more creative, have more energy and their genius is activated. They have purpose and are driven. They have the ability to deeply listen and to support others. They have empathy and a sense of awe, love and gratitude at earth and life itself. And they find the capacity to love, to be compassionate and be forgiving with every ounce of sense-ability they acquire.

Phil: Do you have any suggestions for people as to how they can do/act/work to make change in the world in connection with nature?

Jon: I think there is no more important resource on our planet right now than to awaken to these longings of our autonomic nervous system I mentioned. If people can just use their garden or back yard to awaken their senses and make a practice of it in the same way they might practise meditation or mindfulness. This practice involves sharing stories, even if it's as simple an experience as finding a beetle on a blade of grass. The important thing is to share stories with loved ones so all can express their wonder and joy. All over the world right now people are awakening, helped in part by the Covid-19 pandemic where these very practices are seen to be helping people cope, and find hope.

Phil: What do our leaders and governors need to do most to help make change?

Jon: Our leaders and governors need to support this kind of practice. As Richard Louv says, This is not an 'it would be nice if', it's a human need and should be a birthright. It should be part of the UN declaration that every human has a right to connect to nature in a deeper and profound way, because we know from the science that this is very very good for us. There needs to be space made in people's lives and schools and the curricular standards in our country has to include it.

Bigos (Hunter's Stew)

My mother's family are from Poland and I grew up with their favourite foods. Bigos, or Hunter's Stew, is now a family favourite.

It's good to make a lot of bigos, because everyone who smells it will want it, and you can preserve it for later. I make about 20 litres every time I cook it and give myself a full day to prepare this special dish in stages, listen to my favourite music and invite friends and family to help me cook. We always rest it on the first night and serve and enjoy on the second day. It's much better tomorrow!

Ingredients

2 kg of pork shoulder from local organic butcher source
2 large yellow organic onions
400 g of natural organic bacon
4 kielbasa sausages (from a Polish shop - here in the US they come in lengths of about 40 cm). I sometimes use 12–15 cm bratwursts, or perhaps combine the two.
350 g tomato sauce, made with passata, onion, garlic and oregano
1.6 kg sauerkraut (yes lots of sauerkraut!)
1 big head of organic cabbage
1 kg organic carrots
1.5 kg organic potatoes
Around 40 g of caraway seeds

1 litre of organic vegetable stock (homemade is the best)
1 litre of mushroom stock
1 litre of organic beef bone broth
250 g organic butter
Salt and black pepper to taste
6 bay leaves

Stage one

Get the music on. Gather the team. Take a deep breath and give thanks to my Polish ancestors! Dice the onions and place in melted butter. Finely dice the bacon and add to the onions just as they turn translucent. Sauté slowly, until the bacon crisps up and the onions begin to brown. Add pork shoulder cut into chunks (it will fall apart in the stew, so start with big chunks) and brown.

Stage two

While this is happening, someone is on the grill outside browning the sausages just enough to make them sizzle and to bring out a caramelised flavour. Put them on a tray and let them cool so you can cut them up and add them to the end of stage one above.

Stage three

Bring a big pot of water up to the boil (around 8 litres). Drain the sauerkraut in a colander. (We save the brine solution in jars in the fridge and drink it now and then – it's great for gut health.) Rinse the sauerkraut briefly in water from the tap. Then pour a bit of boiling water over the kraut, stir the kraut in the colander, add more boiling water, then stir again. Repeat three or four times.

Stage four

Mix the sausages, meat and kraut, add the preheated stock. Stir in caraway seeds. When the smell of caraway starts to really enter your sinuses, then maybe you have enough. A lot of caraway. Add all the stock and break the bay leaves into it. Add the chopped cabbage, the potatoes cut into cubes of 4 cm and the carrots in around 2.5 cm chunks. Stir all these ingredients, then top up the pot with water if it's not full. Give it enough heat to bring it to a boil slowly and then cook for at least two hours. Turn it off and let it rest overnight.

The next day serve with rye bread and plenty of room temperature butter for easy spreading.

My family, summer 1960

Early memories of connecting with nature and the great outdoors

I was born on 22nd April 1958 in North Yorkshire, a mile from a village called Gilling in the Vale of Pickering. The place of my birth is set beneath the North York Moors, which offer a harsher, wilder backdrop to the escarpment that then drops into the lightly rolling, hilly-bottomed vale.

There is a typically English, mellow beauty about this part of Yorkshire, with old friendly villages offering community hubs to a thriving farming landscape. The communities around here were largely made up of people working the land. While the driver behind the area's economy was agriculture, the professional classes living there also contributed to the economic wellbeing of the Vale.

Twenty miles to the south was York, with its university, grand cathedral, its chocolate factory and its medieval cobbled streets. Close by was Ampleforth College, a local monastery and private catholic school, where my dad taught English and Drama.

From a very early age and throughout the seasons, the outdoors was a familiar place to me.

Mum was always busy, keeping house for our huge family of 12, while maintaining her life as a prolific author and illustrator of children's books. As tiny children we would often be put outside to play in the garden - a patch of grass bordered by a low wall and the odd flower border. There were no slides or swings - so we got creative. My big brothers once made a slide by placing a huge board up against the nursery window. There was a sandpit, which had grass creeping into it every spring before Mum dug its edges to open the season for mucking about in once again.

As a baby in the pram, I would have been outside a great deal. I'd have experienced so many sounds of nature and the countryside. Birds, wind, tractors, voices, cars, cows mooing. Once out of the pram, there I'd be, sitting on the grass alone, content and safe under Mum's occasional eye from the kitchen window. Clothed in robust old hand-me-down overalls, I was at liberty to grub around. No doubt I ate my fair share of grubs, plants, soil and sand as well. Before I went to school, outdoors was my play area and it provided a rich world of nature discovery.

The dirty hands and face, and, in summer, mucky bare feet too, were a great way to introduce the body to millions of diverse bacteria, challenging the gut and building immunity. Many factors contribute to a strong immune system, but these early years are significant and the more we can offer little ones this chance to play in nature the better resistance to disease they will develop.

There were exciting days of pouring rain when my brothers and I would make a dam on the old farm track that zigzagged all the way down behind the back of the house and round the side past the edge

From a very early age and throughout the seasons, the outdoors was a familiar place to me

important for city children. As climate change challenges us all, learning about and being in nature will play a vital role in finding new ways to live sustainably. The more we expose our children to nature from the start of life, the better they will be equipped to find solutions to the challenges they will face in the future, including potential food shortages. One day humankind may be forced to return to some kind of hunting and gathering, or at least be more involved in a hands-on way to produce food.

It is a tragedy that as humans we have decided we can dominate nature through chemical farming, which degrades the natural order of things. When given the chance, our countryside is abundant and full of health and vitality. Healthy soil is crammed with fabulous, miraculous mycelium, a sort of bacterial colony connecting all life. Mycorrhiza – the symbiotic relationship between fungus and plants – is like a health factory with every tool at its disposal to ensure a good response to all environmental happenings.

Woodlands offer up the chance to discover the intricate web of mycelium as it spreads between trees under the forest leaf mulch. Over centuries, the Chinese have found plenty of fungi that offer incredible healing. I recently used Reishi, which can help with boosting energy, reducing blood pressure and which is known for its anti-cancer potential. Fungi can also help to detoxify the body, eliminate inflammation, and improve your cognitive ability. ℝ

Beyond their medicinal properties, they are also simply delicious to eat. These days you can find so many more varieties to buy in shops including mixed boxes of fungi perfect for the recipe opposite.

of a silage pit. We would add chunks of silage as well as mud and stones, knowing that at some point the water would win. Faster and faster we worked to beat the torrent, all the time learning about the forces of nature, getting soaked, laughing, absorbing the energy of the rain and of the gushing water.

While having fun, I was also learning about nature in all its beauty and wisdom. With a growing confidence in the outdoor world, I was developing a respect for my place within it. From a very young age I was unconsciously gaining an intimate understanding of seasonal patterns.

Part of humanity's onward challenge is to rekindle this connection with nature, and this is especially

Mixed fungi tagliatelle

Many more varieties of fungi are available in good food stores these days. This recipe lends itself to any wild or bought mixed fungi. Be very sure that any wild fungi you have harvested is edible.

Ingredients

At least 100 ml olive oil
150 g to 200 g mixed fresh fungi
2 tablespoons unsalted butter
3 cloves garlic, thinly sliced
2 teaspoons chopped fresh rosemary leaves
½ teaspoon crushed red pepper flakes or a small amount of fresh chopped red chilli
250 ml vegetable stock
400 g dried tagliatelle (you can also use fresh pasta and/or pappardelle)
A bunch of chopped parsley
100 g freshly grated Parmesan cheese, plus more for serving

Method

Bring a large pot of salted water to boil.

While the water is heating, in a large frying pan heat some olive oil until shimmering. Add the mushrooms and cook, stirring, until they wilt and give up their liquid; then increase the heat to boil the liquid away and caramelise the mushrooms (5 to 8 minutes).

Reduce the heat to medium, add the butter and let it melt. Stir in the garlic, rosemary, a pinch each of salt and red pepper and cook just until fragrant (30 seconds).

Add the vegetable stock and simmer until reduced by half. Reduce the heat to very low just to keep warm.

Meanwhile, add the tagliatelle to the boiling water and cook until al dente, maybe 8 minutes or so depending on the type of pasta. When the pasta is ready, transfer it to the sauce, keeping a bit of the pasta water. Drizzle with olive oil, sprinkle with the parsley and toss to coat, adding a little reserved pasta water if it's too dry. It's ready to eat with extra parmesan on top if desired.

Tips

Sparking curiosity

• Teach children about soil bacteria by gently digging under the leaves in woodland to expose white strands of fungus. If you learn about edible wild fungi you might even enjoy eating the fruits of your walk in the woods.

• Find twigs in woodland and, where it's safe, make a small camp fire in a clearing. Children find flames magical and are often happy just to sit and watch them.

• See how many different bugs or birds your children can find on every walk you take in the park or countryside.

• Regularly find silence far away from towns and cars, up in the wild hills. To sit listening to silence is like pure magic.

• Get muddy in nature away from big farms. Ingesting micro amounts of soil is very good for us.

Healing nature

When I was growing up it was obvious to my mum that something about food and farming was capturing my interest and for my 14th birthday in 1972, she bought me a subscription to the Soil Association. Ⓡ

How crazy is this? I really don't get this. I don't read for pleasure. I have zero interest in school and study. And here is this journal called Mother Earth with dense articles on earnest subject matter that I know nothing about. There are no badges, no stickers, no competitions. No club stuff like you might get from a subscription to The Eagle comic. No challenges to suit my 14-year-old mind. Just this brown cover and pictures of old people being very serious about farming.

I always liked to please, so I thanked my mum and set about reading.

What I read drew me into a brand new and fascinating world. I had a sort of 'well, of course!' moment. Here was something that had no relation to school or family. Something that said 'This is how the world of farming could be'. It was full of possibility. It formed a critique of how farming was destroying our natural world as well as our food quality. The soil suddenly became important to me as I started to examine it in relation to its state of health I would frequently grub around in soil looking closely at what life I could see with the naked eye, knowing that under a microscope it would appear to be teeming with life. I discovered that old pasture soil brought up by moles felt so alive and awake, whereas soil in a huge field of chemically grown monocrops was inert and had a foulness about it. Farming against nature is no answer for mankind. We can farm without chemical fertilisers. We can rear animals without cages and without putting antibiotics and hormones in feedstuff. We can farm alongside and in harmony with nature that supports mankind on so many levels.

By the time I was 15 years old I was bewildered emotionally and suffering from depression. No one ever spoke of it. I was prone to outbursts of violent anger and distress. I kept it at bay as best I could through being active in nature. I got a Saturday job on the college farm, feeding animals, mucking out, pulling black oats from wheat crops, sweeping out the granary ready for the next harvest. All this was done with a newly educated eye on how the farming was being done – with all the latest chemicals and machinery to maximise yields and dominate nature.

At home I found places to be alone in old pasture fields, where I picked wild flowers and dried them. I kept a diary on good days, which was little more than a few lines of searching, but it played a part in soothing my screaming heart.

> **Let nature help young people understand life and allow it to support them**

School life was pretty hellish. I hated the boys who trashed me when it suited them. One day, feeling very low and anxious, the boy who sat behind me on the school bus knuckled me on the head over and over again. This was a regular occurrence and to this day I don't understand why I always sat right in front of him. Anyway, that morning I flipped, stood up and pummelled him with blinding rage. We were pulled apart by the driver and other children and he never did it again. Reflecting on this now it is obvious I was screaming for help. I was heading into my last year in that school. I would sometimes go in just for registration and then walk down the old railway line to Helmsley to drink in the Feathers Hotel. Later, I would walk in the grounds of Helmsley Castle and sit with nature and allow it to soothe me. Then I would catch the school bus home on its way back through.

Three bits of secondary school that were positive for me were domestic science, woodwork and pottery, all tactile and allowing me to use my hands, which made me feel safe and confident. Of course, boys weren't supposed to like domestic science and I was teased – so that had to go.

School came to an end for me after I was sent to the headmaster for throwing a board rubber at the music teacher. He had asked a pair of twins who were stone deaf to come out to the front and sing. This was clearly done for the class to laugh at but it made me want to cry. Filled with rage, I deliberately turned my back on the teacher to look out of the window and ignore the class. He told me to turn around and when I didn't he threw the board rubber at me. I picked it up and violently threw it back at him. The headmaster was not interested in me at all. He just had his job to do and wanted to cane me on the hands. I was done with this place in every cell of my being and told him he was not going to f*****g cane me and he could f**k off. I walked out of the school and down to Helmsley again, got drunk and then went home.

I said nothing to anyone. A week later Mum and Dad got a letter suggesting that I leave. Underneath the surface I was screaming for help. Teenagers often find it hard to let those around them know what's going on, in part because often they don't really know themselves. I see such a huge gain from parents taking adolescents out into the wildest parts of nature to be found. Words are then not needed. Let nature help young people understand life and allow it to support them. This is best done without others so they don't feel peer pressure to behave in a particular way, which can mean they miss out half of what nature can offer. It's the alone time that matters, perhaps with a parent or mentor around for support. The deeper the nature experience the better.

Escape to the hills

Malaig Harbour, 1970s

Despite my silence, it must have been clear to my family I was troubled as my older brothers Barny and Mark invited me on a trip up to Scotland. We travelled to Edinburgh and on up to Pitlochry to visit Lois, a friend and flame (probably) of Barny's. A walk up Ben Vrackie was the first time in my life that I had experienced such silence. The only sounds were the grouse. I remember sitting in wonder and bliss at such an unusual sense of stillness. It was overwhelming.

A day later on the train to Mallaig over on the west coast we saw an eagle, a sight not uncommon then, but now extremely rare. After stocking up on basic provisions we went to find a place to pitch our tent. We camped on a wet hillside and it rained all day and all night. Early in the morning we got up to a dry sky with a little watery sunshine and tramped down to the harbour. Barny asked one of the fishermen who had just landed a load of herring if we could buy a few. For next to nothing, we left the harbour with a dozen super-fresh herring. Barny found garlic and lemon in the greengrocer and Mark bought some bread and butter. On the way back to camp we gutted and

After much smoke and blowing we had ourselves a warm fire and pan-fried the fish to perfection

washed the herring in a mountain stream. Back at camp Mark and I found enough rather damp wood to make a fire while Barny got ready with the food and plates. My job was to rig up a string close to the fire to dry out our wet socks that were soon steaming away in the heat. Boy scout training had at least taught us how to make fires in difficult circumstances. After much smoke and blowing we had ourselves a warm fire and Barny pan-fried the fish to perfection. That meal was truly sublime. It was total delight down to the washing of the pans and plates in the stream. Barny and Mark were often almost hysterical with laughter throughout the holiday at their private little jokes, which went over my young head. I still wonder if Mum had words with Barny about taking me, but I will always remember it with gratitude, knowing that he and Mark looked after their, somewhat troubled, baby brother.

The best feasts often involve a combination of elements, as this one did: story, provenance, simplicity and, of course, hunger! I hope you can achieve at least some of these with this simple recipe.

Simply herring

The most important thing about oily fish is freshness. Find out from a fishmonger when they are coming in and buy them and eat them that day.

Take each herring and cut from the belly to the tail inside, use your hands to push the fish outwards to flatten them into 2 fillets still attached along the back. Pull out the backbone. If you find this tricky get your fishmonger to do it for you, but watch them so you can do it next time. It's not difficult and all part of building confidence and fun around cooking from scratch.

For around 8 herring, mix together 1 tablespoon salt, 1 teaspoon sugar and ½ teaspoon freshly ground pepper. You will also need some lemon wedges.

Sprinkle your seasoning over the insides of the fish and leave for about 45 minutes with the skin facing upwards. Grill them on both sides for no more than a few minutes each side and serve with lemon squeezed over. They go really well with some mixed garden leaf salad and brown toast. Also you can leave to cool, take out any further bones of a size worth bothering with and serve with a ribbon pasta with added parsley, lots of lemon and some olive oil.

Nature's signposts to health

Throughout my life I have seen first hand the enormous impact that working on the land can offer people. If we are ever to make humankind's life on this planet sustainable it will be because we will have become more connected to nature. Mother Earth and nature is where we come from and where we will return to. It's what we walk on and inhabit everyday of our life. Holding the intention to care for it is for sure good for our own wellbeing.

When I was struggling with depression as a young man, my work on the land was a daily life saver. Mother Earth was always unquestioning and loyal, always there to catch my soul and soothe me.

We are facing an immense challenge – that of ensuring that nature is there to be enjoyed at all. There are still vast amounts of wild and wonderful land on earth. Yet, the amount of time and resources we spend in it is limited by our city living and culture.

Humankind seems hell bent on journeying towards a time and place where natural life is a side show at best. It is possible that the Covid-19 pandemic has awakened us enough to shift this way of thinking and being. Perhaps nature will become more central and we can learn to trust a little more that we are but an outcrop of it.

It was early April 2019 and I was out walking. I came to some big fields which were part of a local dairy farm in the Chew Valley. The field was sodden and smothered in cow slurry. It looked very sick - as if it had been poisoned and then drowned. The only sound was of crows hanging around the back of the nearby monster-size cowsheds. They were scavenging on death. I had a sense that nature had no way to thrive and so was responding with decay and foul smells.

Later that same day, I walked across another field. This was a permanent pasture on part of an organic farm. It was also wet, due to the winter rains, but was healthy and open with a good mat of grass, clover and meadow herbage. There were signs of worms everywhere. I noticed the birds and I could sense that nature was in relative balance – vital and healthy. My spirits lifted.

If most of what we grow is produced while crushing nature and supressing sickness with chemicals then the health of food produced in this way is inevitably compromised. Our own health and wellbeing is directly affected. If we nourish our soils and allow

The healing power of a walk in nature

Minestrone

This is such a delicious, hearty and versatile soup.

Choose whatever veg you like but always include, onion, garlic and carrot. Add perhaps 200 g of other root veg and 150 g of greens of some kind. A couple of sticks of celery is a great addition. Heat a large heavy-bottomed pan with several tablespoons of olive oil over a medium heat. Finely chop the garlic and onion and sauté. Finely chop all the other veg, adding roots first, then 5 minutes later add the rest of the veg except greens. Continue cooking for another 10 minutes.

If you are using potatoes then add now with some beans, either leftovers or from a tin. You can even get away with baked beans. Add a tin of chopped tomatoes, then add some vegetable stock or water and a stock cube.

Put a lid on the pan and simmer for about 15 minutes. Now taste for seasoning. Add salt and pepper to taste.

Now add some pasta. Kids like alphabet pasta that's easy to get or any pasta that is fine and quick to cook. Add the chopped greens and cook for a further 8 minutes, or until the pasta is cooked.

Some fresh summer herbs are the last addition. Chopped parsley or chervil is great, or a bit of ripped basil.

Holding the intention to care for nature is for sure good for our own wellbeing

our natural world to flourish it will feed not only our physical wellbeing, but also our spirit and our place in the cosmos.

Of course, we lead busy lives and we feel we need some easy solutions to help us. However, we are paying a huge price for this assistance. Every element of our food chain impacts on our whole health. Our bodies flourish or sicken depending on the food that we eat; our emotional being is nourished by nature's health. Our spirits lift to a place of joy when we encounter the wonder of nature while fear and depression creep in if we are surrounded by the ugliness of sick land.

One way of supporting the health of the land as well as ourselves - mind, body and spirit - is to choose to buy and eat organic fruit and vegetables.

An organic box direct from a farm can be a true gift, abundant in nature's health. It has been produced with care for our soil, which is critical to our health. The love and attention given to the growing, harvesting, preparing and delivering this box of nutritious food fills it with life-enhancing energy. Good for the body, good for the soul! If it's possible for you, choose a box from a small box scheme that is mostly doing its own growing, rather than a national one.

Enough mess and disconnection

It is human nature to want to progress. These advances give us a sense of purpose and security. I wonder if we will ever stop working to progress to make life more convenient and easier? I see this as humanity's greatest challenge. When is it time to say 'enough'? When will we be satisfied? When will we be strong enough to accept risk as a human condition and stop trying to de-risk life itself?

We are now developing drone bees to pollinate plants. In our attempts to make food production easier and more secure we have inadvertently killed most of our pollinating bees. Now progress has provided us with the technology to replace the bees we have killed. Progress through science and technology may not be actually making things easier, but far more complex, breeding a sense of insecurity and a lack of basic trust in others. At what point might we be able to say 'I know I can make life "easier" and so stay secure but I actively choose not to do so.'?

There are consequences to every action and even the tiniest of these have an impact on life on earth. Every time I walk on the ground, something at a micro level dies. Every time I get in my car, life is lost. Yet we can choose to live with light footsteps on the earth, and this starts I believe with love of oneself. Maybe from this we are in a stronger place to choose a path that heals earth and enables us to live with and maybe celebrate the inherent insecurity of life. Often our most treasured or rich moments in life are when we have let go.

Our soils are in crisis, our birds, bees and wildlife are plummeting in numbers. Our biodiversity has never been so endangered. Our health, by some measures, has never been so poor the world over. Our true happiness has never been so under threat. The self-confidence around what it is to be truly human is ailing badly. Our mental wellbeing and peace within ourselves is at an all-time low.

Humanity is lost and hurting, but we are also extraordinarily good in our ability to create new paths, to rise up to challenge and be creative in order to ensure our survival. In this lies our potential for healing. The great awakening is taking place every day across the world.

Tips

Living well with nature

- Seek out inconvenience and realise it can make life more fun.

- Walk on the ground every day. Not just tarmac, concrete and carpets, but grass and earth paths. This helps you connect directly with the energy of the earth.

- Find a sit spot outside somewhere even if it's a back yard and just ponder on the nature around you. Listen and nature will let you know how close she is.

- Find gratitude for what you have. Small things can make such a big difference to our day.

Find a sit spot outside and ponder on the nature around you

John and Phil at the
Community Farm

Reconnect and return to the land

Before human beings began to farm we were few in number. We were living within the limits of our environment. We were spiritually much more connected to the land, the sky and the stars, indeed the universe, as well as the mystery of life.

We spent all our lives connected to nature in a way we can only dream of now. We would have been relatively unquestioning and confident within our place in the cosmos.

Farming led to exploitation of land and people. It put power and money in the hands of the few. We forgot to check back at every move we made to be sure that what we were doing was balanced and connected

to our place in the cosmos. This is what sustainable means. A positive impact on our ability to live within the means of, and with true connection to, Planet Earth.

Yet we can still make this connection today. Indeed, every day many of us experience positive human connection.

One way back to the roots of what it is to be human and to heal the trauma caused by 'progress' is to reconnect with our food and our soils and know we are truly nourished by them when we nurture nature. Our great world challenge is to shift all farming from an industrial to human scale and with no ownership of land. Millions of people involved in food production offer us the best solution, with the soil, nature and the mystery of the cosmos as our master. Human beings could be living as nature's servants, knowing and appreciating that its generosity knows no bounds.

A truly global campaign to return to the land and tend to nature and soil as our first love and commitment would I believe have the greatest ever impact on humanity's ability to be at peace with itself and with the planet and thereby take us on a journey to better health.

We must shift all farming from an industrial to a human scale

A University for Life

Our education system in the West is in some ways not fit for purpose. It is underfunded and it drives a curriculum that lacks the skills our young people truly need to face the life ahead of them. Yet, preparing them to help repair our culture and our farming cannot be the responsibility of schools alone. All of us can be more involved with the mentoring and teaching of our children.

Our ability to mend our world will be best pursued in a joined-up way where we pay equal attention to both land and food as well as our interconnectedness.

We are now at a crossroads for humanity. The climate crisis and the Covid-19 pandemic demonstrate all is not well. We are rising up and taking to the streets to say 'enough'. We are frightened and see that we must change and we must do it now.

I think it's time to build a 'University for Life' as a place we can all attend.

There are thousands and thousands of inspiring teachers out there who already teach and support others to foster better community, better farming, better interconnectedness and better leaders. Could we form a global alliance between all these teachers and leaders to develop a curriculum that becomes a blueprint for a new world order?

A new way could offer us a better way

Our so-called leaders of the world are in fact holders of the power to protect the broken status quo. We cannot expect that simply demanding change will bring it about, we can 'be the change'. We can build a global network to redesign how we want to live on the crust of this planet in this, our time.

The founding purpose of a University for Life is very simply to re-humanise humanity. This could be done through nature connection, land work, community healing and the healing of self. I believe the will is out there across the world to make something happen that has never happened before. Why? Because we have never been in such a global crisis. We all know the ice is melting. It's do or die.

In just a few months at the start of 2020 we have seen a global shift in behaviour of great magnitude. While lives have been lost in thousands to the virus, we have also reduced our CO_2 impact on the planet. This has allowed nature to start to creep back in and for people to start to breathe clean air again. We did it in a matter of weeks. The system will have us rush back to economic growth as fast as possible. Yet a new way could offer us a better way. Our global thinkers and activists have one of the best opportunities ever to bring into being a network of learning that would penetrate every single community and every single school.

My plea is for us all to think and to connect with others and form new ways that will become a force for change. The foundations for change we already have can now be built on fast. This is the time, this is our time. Please connect with me via the Better Food website with your ideas of how we can make this happen – together.

Mya-Rose Craig
Environmentalist

Mya-Rose Craig, blogs as Birdgirl and is a prominent young birder, passionate about nature, saving the planet and fighting for equal access to nature for all.

It is essential for humankind's future survival that we save Nature's species from extinction. Without our beautiful, varied and individual insects, birds, animals and fish, biodiversity will collapse. We will be left to cope without abundant food sources and our ecosystems will be at best fragile although, in reality, more likely to be totally decimated. The answer is simple but the sacrifices seem too difficult for our globalised world and capitalist societies and governments to enact.

We must stop plundering the planet, treating its resources as ours to take. Instead we must start respecting the environment as most indigenous peoples do. We must implement sustainable farming, so that wildlife can live alongside it rather than nature paying the price.

We need to move away from industrialised farming, instead implementing practices that used to be common, as promoted by the Nature Friendly Farming Network, such as leaving set-aside and stopping the use of poisonous insect-killing pesticides. We need to stop practices that destroy habitats such as driven grouse shooting moors. We must replant native trees in our now barren uplands. And we have to stop persecuting our native animals such as foxes, deer and badger.

We need to stop trawling our seas, stop overfishing and the use of long lines, and start allowing sea creatures to recover. If we create huge protected areas with no-catch zones, numbers will come back.

Where globalisation has caused habitats to be destroyed, we must re-wild to support nature's return, such as the reforestation of palm oil plantations in Borneo to prevent Orangutan extinction and regenerating the Amazon rainforest. Finally, we need to stop the earth warming more than two degrees, which will kill our oceans, kill our land with drought and pit human existence against all other living things. We must do this by forcing governments and big businesses to make drastic changes to reduce carbon emissions and by planting trillions of trees.

Bangladeshi tarka dhal

My Nanu's recipe

Scoop 2 mugs of red lentils into a large pan, wash and drain away water 3-4 times or until water runs clear. This part is often boring but very important for the quality of the dhal at the end.

Fill a pan with boiling water, add ½ teaspoon each of turmeric and salt (if used).

Put pan on high heat until the water starts to bubble, then turn down to a medium heat. Use a large slatted spoon to skim the froth from the top of the water and occasionally stir to make sure no lentils are sticking to the bottom.

After about 30 minutes, turn off the heat and use a potato masher to mash the lentils.

Five minutes before the dhal is served, make the tarka. Melt butter in a frying pan and add crushed garlic (both to taste), fry and add 3 chillies (optional).

Add the tarka to the dhal and give it a quick stir.

Done! It tastes best fresh but also stores/freezes very well.

> **"**
> We have the ability to create new paths, to rise up to challenge and be creative in order to ensure our survival

Resources
Better for nature

Organisations for better nature

8 Shields
8shields.org

Nature Friendly Farming Network
www.nffn.org.uk

The Soil Association
www.soilassociation.org

Books

Davies, Geoff (2019) *Economy, Society, Nature*, World Economics Association.

Louv, Richard (2010) *Last Child in the Woods: Saving our children from nature-deficit disorder*, Atlantic Books.

Macartney, Mac (2018) *The Children's Fire: Heart song of a people*, Practical Inspiration Publishing.

Norman Powell, M (2001) *Ingwe*, Owlinked Media.

Powell, Martin (2013) *Medicinal Mushrooms: The essential guide*, Mycology Press.

Stamets, Paul (2004) *Mycelium Running: A guide to healing the planet through gardening with gourmet and medicinal mushrooms*, Ten Speed Press

Young, Jon, Hass, Ellen, McGown, Evan (2010) *Coyote's Guide to Connecting with Nature*, Owlinked Media.

Articles, blogs, web

Gorissen, Leen 'Why your immune system needs a forest', www.naturalintelligence.info/post/why-your-immune-system-needs-a-forest?fbclid=IwAR2Uqfw7ojFUlPK0VvE07s1Lvf23aL9be8ANplh3Uj0VswM2IdXXYMqoJsY (accessed 8 June 2020)

Nagdeve, Meenakshi 'Cancer: Treatments & Home Remedies', www.organicfacts.net/home-remedies/home-remedies-for-cancer.html (accessed 8 June 2020)

https://www.independent.co.uk/life-style/health-and-families/health-news/supermarkets-care-nothing-for-our-health-thats-our-job-9537729.html (accessed 25 May 2020)

The Royal Society (2001) 'The role of land carbon sinks in mitigating world climate change', royalsociety.org/-/media/Royal_Society_Content/policy/publications/2001/9996.pdf

Young, Richard (2014) 'What meat to eat?', sustainablefoodtrust.org/articles/the-meat-debate-red-meat/ (accessed 9 June 2020)

Better cook and eat

Putting food back into the heart and soul of humanity

Food glorious food! It lies at the heart of all we do in the world. We live because we eat, we celebrate with food, we build communities through food. It can be sensational, absorbing, delicious, beautiful, powerful. And of course nutritious. The food we eat is at its best when made from fresh raw ingredients that come from the soil via plants or animals and not via laboratories and factories. Food at its best is full of vitality and soul because it originates from soil that is full of the same.

Since before the tin can was invented, we have striven to make food more and more convenient. Following the Second World War there has been a cheap food policy operating in the United Kingdom. This has led us down a route that marketeers can exploit to their hearts' content. Now, food quality has declined immeasurably to the point where much of our food does nothing to nourish us, but rather poisons us instead.

The world is waking up to the facts. We are not feeding ourselves well and the systems of farming we created to produce 'cheap' food are causing untold damage. It's time to reclaim our food and make it meaningful once again. We can do this by taking time to source it locally, to cook it with love and to sit down and share it with others whenever possible. Ultimately this requires us to slow it all down and have a lot more fun making, and eating it.

Barny Haughton's omelette

In writing this recipe again for Phil after all these years, I wanted to look at the act of cooking from a particular perspective; not to think about provenance or the why you do this in such a way or the chemistry or even taste, but its physicality, the colours and sounds and movements... just to be with what's going on.

When I first wrote this recipe 12 years ago, it began: *The first thing you need to do to make an omelette is to get out of bed.*

At that time, every morning, I was struggling to do just that. I could see no beauty in the world. The words people spoke had no meaning. Days were barely different from nights. Food tasted of nothing. Depression comes in many forms, but one most people who suffer from it recognise is its capacity to be like an anaesthetic. To disconnect you from feeling and from the world around you. And if food – that most visceral and immediate and primary of all life's experiences – is also your work, the everyday business of being a chef - writing menus, preparing vegetables, sharing ideas with the other chefs in the kitchen, tasting and smelling things as you cook them and –

especially somehow – at the pass arranging ingredients on the plate, becomes fairly surreal.

But I went on cooking. I went on chopping onions and sweating them down till they were soft and sweet and adding other things and putting whatever I had made on to plates for people to eat. I didn't think about it or like it, I just did it. The act of cooking became a kind of therapy. Sometime after this, when beauty had returned to the world, I began to see that cooking could, in a certain context, also be a meditation and that making an omelette, the most simple of all dishes, could illustrate this perfectly.

It takes five minutes. You need to do it on your own and in silence.

You need three eggs, a frying pan and some heat. You need a bowl and a fork, a knife and a chopping board. And a warm plate to put the omelette on. And some herbs, perhaps tarragon, dill and chives – because this is going to be a herb omelette – salt and pepper, a nob of butter and some olive oil. And we're going to put a little fresh goat's cheese in this omelette too.

Have everything ready.

The herbs on the chopping board, the crumbly white goat's cheese and the green olive oil... the light through the kitchen window. Allowing a little time to pass...

Break the three eggs into the bowl, add the salt and pepper and a swirl of green olive oil.
Chop the herbs and beat them with the fork into the egg mix
Add a little more olive oil in the almost smoky hot pan
Slip the egg mixture swiftly in one movement into the pan
Sizzle for 4 seconds, beating gently with a fork
One, two, three, four
Sprinkle the crumbly white goat's cheese onto the mix
One, two, three
Tip the pan slightly away from you and with the fork, fold the mix from the far edge
Back towards you
Letting the liquid egg follow gravity back down the slope of the pan
One, two, three, four
While still sloppy on the upper side and just brown underneath, fold the mix
Away from you
One, two, three
Gently over onto a warm plate.

Phil talked to...
Barny Haughton

Barny Haughton is a chef, teacher and food educator. He opened his first restaurant in Bristol in 1988 and went on to run two others, the third of which was Bordeaux Quay.

Barny founded Square Food Foundation in 2011, a community cookery school which teaches people from all backgrounds and of all ages and abilities to cook good food and to better understand the role food plays in every aspect of life.

Phil: What is important to you about food and cooking?

Barny: In the end, the thing I always come back to and which is central to understanding food education, is personal food identity: one person's relationship with food.

And what most powerfully tells the story of anyone's relationship with food is memories. Even when they are no longer quite clear or, if others have a different memory of the same event. Food ties you to the memory. It is the portal through which you find them again. It tells you who you are now and were then and who those other people were too. It is one story of your life.

This memory you will remember well, Phil. I often wonder why it remains so particularly vivid and precious. When we talk about it now, thinking back to it, there is a small question mark over whether they were mackerel or herring. But what I do remember was the damp grey early morning sunlight on the boats which had just come in and the busy harbourside and the fish, slender and bright flashed silver and blue, the colours of the sea itself,

and so many of them, more clouds than heaps, still rather than dead, in big white plastic boxes, the men moving between the boxes, shouting over the noise of engines, about their work so ordinary to them and so mesmerising and unknown to us. And the smell of diesel oil and fish and the sea.

I think they just gave us the fish. Or did we pay for them? In any case, a little later we were back at our campsite, a sloping bit of ground of rocks and heather - you would think three country boys might have found a better place to pitch a tent - and had lit a fire, made coffee and were cooking the fish over it and eating it with our hands, picking the flesh off their little frames, spitting out the bones.

Did we have lemon? Or salt? Did we gut the fish first? Was that Skye or Mull over the water? What were we three thinking about at the time?

Phil: Do you have any suggestions for people as to how they can do/act/work to make change in the world around food?

Barny: Make an omelette.

Phil: What do our leaders and governors need to do most to help make change in the world?

Barny: Make an omelette.

66
What a joy it was... to be sent off to explore and bring back the bounties of the countryside

Foraging

Today, if I smell a puffball, it takes me back to the first time I found one in a field below our house under some old crab apple trees. I took it home and Mum fried it in butter for our tea. From then on, I knew that wild food could be good. Those same trees within the same season also gave us crab apple jelly. Then close by would have been blackberries for pies and jams and rosehips for syrup to ward off winter colds. By the age of five, I understood that the natural world played a part in feeding us seasonal delights. All had to be picked and my elder siblings would all have got out there to gather the harvest in. What a joy it was simply to be sent off to pick, to explore and bring back the bounties of the countryside.

Our primary school, St Benedict's in Ampleforth village, was two miles from home. I remember one teacher in particular, Mrs Ward, because she was very warm and caring, but also because she took us on walks around the fields to explore the hedgerows. She would ask us the names of birds and flowers. Once, we picked crab apples and took them back to the school kitchen to make crab apple jelly. We all got a little taste before it was put in jars.

The next day she got us all to save the top of the milk given to us at morning break. This would have been unpasteurised milk, left on the school doorstep at air temperature, allowing cream to rise to the top quickly. From that cream we made butter, all being given a turn to churn it. Mrs Ward asked the school cook to make us some little scones and we ate these warm with our own butter and crab apple jelly. As six- or seven-year-olds, you can probably imagine how happy that made us on that day!

Giant puffballs

You will find puffballs in August and September in old meadows where grazing animals have recently been - never on recently cultivated ground. I have also never found them in the same place two years running, but this may be just coincidence.

Ingredients

A puffball (or you can use any other fungi)
Olive oil or butter to fry
1 large chopped onion and 2 cloves garlic chopped finely or crushed
A squeeze of lemon juice
Salt and pepper

Method

Cut the puffball into slices a good centimetre thick. Add the onion and garlic to a pan of gently melted butter or olive oil if you prefer, add a pinch of salt to taste, and leave to braise slowly for about 15 minutes. Remove the onions to a side dish then gently fry the puffball slices for about 3 minutes each side, adding a little more butter or oil if needed. Return the onions and garlic to the pan and add a squeeze of lemon. Serve with a sprinkle of chopped parsley, a few turns of a pepper grinder and a little salt if desired.

This goes well with mashed potato, an egg and some greens. Buckwheat works beautifully alongside it too. If you haven't cooked buckwheat, try it. It's a lovely grain. Put 40 g per person in a heavy pan on high heat for a few minutes moving it about to stop it scorching, then add just enough water to cover and turn it right down. Add a little tamari soy sauce as the water begins to reduce. Ideally you want to cook it to almost dry, which is not always easy to judge, but if necessary you can add a little hot water.

Coming home in winter to milk and dripping on toast

I have childhood memories of freezing cold Yorkshire winters. In particular, the winter of 1963 is remembered for its chill factor and its length. It was so cold that the sea froze in parts. The North East Riding of Yorkshire was blasted by cold winds taking temperatures down to as low as -20c. After cold adventures in snow and ice we would arrive home, wellies and hand-me-down tweed jackets off. Time to warm through and enjoy some comfort food. Dripping toast with Marmite. Mum's legendary homemade brown bread: moist and dense, toasted on the Aga and spread with beef dripping from the butcher's, topped with Marmite. (These days I love it with miso instead.) All swilled down with a mug of milk. Not just any milk, this was milk from the farm dairy just 200 yards away, ladled out of big churns whenever we needed it.

Wheat is nourishing when grown in healthy soil

The milk came down a pipeline through some cooler grids and into the huge churns in the dairy. At the age of four it was all I could do to get the jug ladle in and out of the churn without spilling it. Nobody seemed to mind when I left a mess on the floor – it was always so wet anyway. The best days were when the milk lorry hadn't been and the churns formed lots of cream at the top. Then the morning cornflakes with plenty of creamy milk and brown sugar were extra yummy!

Our daily bread

Bread is such a sacred food, eaten by the world's people since early farming began. Even if, as children, we envied our friends' daily consumption of Mothers Pride® for tea, today I am so grateful for not being allowed these sliced white loaves. The factory methods for making bread cuts out all the proving time and adds loads of preservatives to ensure it keeps. The reality is this method, along with industrial chemically grown wheat, has left some in our nation with an intolerance to wheat and bread with its very low-grade nutritional values. To this day when I smell factory bread being toasted, I am reminded of the chemicals they use on farms to preserve silage.

In fact, today's manufacturing technology makes bread with a longer shelf life by the use of chemicals. Various preservatives including potassium sorbate, sodium benzoate, both used to preserve silage for cattle, have also been used to inhibit mould. (Knicky & Spörndly, 2009)

Fabulously healthy and delicious bread made from old varieties of wheat grown in fertile soils can nourish us in both body and soul. Now, good bread

Dripping toast

You can make your own dripping by buying the right sort of beef fat from your butcher and simply rendering it down very slowly in an oven heated to about 150 deg C. Three hours later, pour all the liquid into an old pudding bowl and let it set. It will keep for months in the fridge.

The bread is up to you, but try making a loaf of my mum's wholemeal bread. See page 101 for the recipe. Toast some of this (if you are lucky enough to have a Rayburn or Aga, use it). Spread a good amount of dripping on your toast and then add miso, Marmite or any other yeast extract. You can also try gomasio, a mix of seeds roasted with salt and ground.

Bread is a sacred food

is more available than it has been for several decades. Sadly, supermarkets continue to sell 'fake' good bread. You know the ones with names like 'multi seed', 'natural wholemeal' and so on, names that conceal the fact that most of them are just factory preserved loaves with added foods to make them seem healthy. Bread in supermarkets is positioned to be cheap. The more air they can add, the better value we think we're getting.

Growing good wheat requires a lot of soil health and available nutrients. Ploughing is used in the main in order to prepare the soil for a wheat crop. There are more and more farmers converting to no-plough, which can significantly reduce CO_2 release as well as reduce the use of tractor fuel.

The bread we ate as children was made with organic stoneground wholemeal flour that Mum bought direct from Pimhill, a farm belonging to the Mayall family, which had been organic since 1949. Also from Pimhill Farm came porridge oats for our breakfast and to this day I believe these to be the best organic porridge oats on the market.

Red meat can be good for our planet and health

I t is time to drop all farming methods that are not truly nature friendly and organic. With climate impact and the need to feed the world populations we must take great care of our farmland and our soils. When we do work with nature, our UK climate can grow lots of grass, trees and herbage producing fantastic healthy beef and lamb with zero use of grains and our farms can be abundant and vital.

Over 95% of beef is reared with the help of grains and soya. Along with current breeding methods to ensure little fat and fast growth this results in an unnatural product. The system fells rainforests and grows GM soya to feed cattle in feedlots on a vast industrial scale.

Yet, there is another way. Beef and any red meat eaten in moderate quantities can be very good for you and the planet. In the UK, you can choose local, organic, grass-fed beef or lamb. It is the only kind that is genuinely very good for you as well as for the environment. Rearing cows and sheep for meat with low density stocking rates on good permanent pasture is helping convert grassland into a healthy diet for cattle as well as producing healthy meat for us. It helps keep our soils full of life and mycelium, playing a vital role in a mixed farm's fertility and diversity. Good pasture can also lock carbon into the soil in huge amounts, which could make a vast difference to global carbon emission levels. According to the Royal Society (2001), if global farmland was managed better it could lock up 10 billion tons of carbon per year. And Carbon Farmers America estimate that if we increase global farmland carbon by 1.6% the problem of climate change would be solved. Ⓡ

Some may argue that methane from cows negates all this good farming, but work by the Sustainable Food Trust shows clearly that, for the UK, which is a nation blessed with a great deal of grass, the best diet will include beef, lamb and dairy from grass pastures. All the while wildlife can thrive. Methane also dissipates in less than 10 years and has been found to have been over-calculated by a factor of 4. Livestock in fact only contributes 4% to climate with the current farming system, which we know can be so much better. It's a complex issue - for more insights see Richard Young's article. Ⓡ

> Choose local, organic, grass-fed beef or lamb. It is the only kind that is genuinely very good for you

Beef in the bog

You will find an overwhelming number of recipes for boeuf bourguignon, for beef casserole and daube of beef and so on. So much is written about the importance of method and ingredients and how it 'ought to be done'. However, we can also just enjoy good simple ingredients cooked in a method that brings out the best in the beef cuts we use.

Go to the butcher's, farm shop, or good retailer where you can buy organic grass-fed beef. Ask for a cheaper cut, but not brisket for this dish – you could use shin, or some braising cuts. You might want 1 kg per 4 to 5 people, but adjust quantities to suit your numbers and appetites. The dish also keeps for a week in the fridge.

Ingredients

1 kg beef, cut into cubes of around 2.5 cms or more
100 g salt pork lardons or streaky bacon if fine
2 or 3 onions diced or 300 g shallots are very lovely instead
300 g carrots diced
3 cloves garlic crushed
A handful of mushrooms
A good squeeze of tomato puree
Half bottle red wine – any decent table wine will do
A slice of orange peel if you like, skin without the pith. It adds a lovely top flavour
A couple of bay leaves, some mixed herbs, fresh is wonderful but dry is just fine, salt, pepper, juniper berries if you have a few, and a stick of celery doesn't go amiss if you have one. Heat the oven to 160 deg C

Method

Use a heavy bottom pan if possible to fry off the lardons or bacon until crispy. Take them out, leaving the oil and add chunks of beef and brown on all sides. I know it's tempting to add all the beef, but it's much better if you do no more chunks than will cover the bottom of the pan with a bit of space for turning. Place all beef with the lardons in a bowl once fried or browned. Add a little wine to the pan to deglaze and pour over the fried meats.

Give your pan a bit of a wipe and then add some olive oil.

Fry the onions slowly until they are soft, add garlic and herbs and fry a little longer. Now replace the meat along with the carrots, mushrooms, tomato puree and orange peel if using. Season with salt and pepper and add a few juniper berries. Pour in your red wine, bring to a simmer and stir gently for a couple of minutes. Put it in the oven and leave for at least 3 hours. (If your pan doesn't go in the oven you will need to transfer the mixture to a casserole dish.)

The meat will be soft but not falling apart, the carrots will have absorbed lots of flavour and added their sweetness to the whole dish.

Serve with beautifully mashed potato and greens.

A family supper in the
caravan, Lothlorien, 1975

Saying our thank yous

Honour your occasional meal of healthy organic meat for the sake of a good balanced diet by remembering where it comes from. Let's pay homage to the beautiful animal from which we took a life to feed us. When I was a child we used to say grace before eating. While I am not remotely interested in following any religious doctrine these days, ritual and prayer in some form are important to me and sometimes I take a moment to mentally give thanks to our beautiful earth for feeding me and for a sentient being sacrificed for my wellbeing.

All life is sacred and maybe we can treat all food with a greater sense of this when we eat from earth's bountiful garden. Once we were wild and simply ate what we could to keep us alive and healthy. For sure it was mostly plant based but hunting and grubs offered protein from living creatures. Hunting can be something that is a wonder to behold in nature. Within all nature there is no greed, but simply a deep connection to being part of a whole system and fighting to stay fit and keep your place in the harsh beauty of the natural world.

I believe that the world is here to support and provide, and that may mean berries and nuts, it may mean yak's milk, it may mean fish, it may mean wild meat, or farmed meat. Whatever it is, let's consume it with honour, respect, celebration and joy.

Chickens, eggs and pork

Chicken has become our most widely eaten meat. We have been encouraged to eat it as a low fat and healthy option. Poultry is highly dependent on grains and beans for its protein and has been massively intensified to produce very cheap meat that costs our environment in hidden ways.

A chicken's life is short, but organic birds live the longest and grow the slowest. They taste better, lose less weight in cooking and, most important of all, because the feed they eat is grown with no chemicals it offers our bees and worms a better chance to flourish and improve the health of nature and therefore us. I know that there are many people who may like to eat organic all the time but just can't afford to do so and free range is certainly a step in the right direction. No matter how deep or shallow our pockets, if we think about animal welfare, climate impact and our bees, then we will likely eat it less often and enjoy it all the more as a treat.

With both table birds and eggs it is best for all if we can choose organic. It's also important to find out more about the farm and what they mean by free range and/or organic so it is a fully informed and conscious choice that we are making.

Pigs

Pigs are the most wonderful creatures and great converters of food waste to protein-dense food. They are intelligent and if given the right environment are friendly and clean. I recently discovered after reading *Wilding* by Isabella Tree that pigs can dive in water and have been seen bringing up fresh water mussels, opening them with their trotters and teeth and eating them.

During and after the World Wars, pigs were kept in small numbers on farms. Many people just had the one pig, fed mostly on scraps and harvest waste. Although many of those pigs were in small pens, which did not allow them to express much natural behaviour, feeding swill (waste from hotels, etc) was commonplace and a very efficient way to recycle waste. Keeping pigs in this way was banned in 2001 due to foot and mouth disease. With all the technology available to ensure great hygiene it is a shame we have never returned to making pig feed out of our waste.

Modern pig farming is a disgraceful and truly shocking industrial mess and by any humane standards the meat is not in any way fit for consumption. Pork is a food to celebrate when farmed and reared really well and if done using lots of waste foods is also environmentally much better. Current legislation does not allow us to legally do it in a way that is good for the environment. (See *The Guardian* article in resources written by restaurateur Thomasina Miers who co-founded The Pig Idea, a campaign to lift the ban on feeding food waste to pigs.)

A chicken's life is short, but organic birds live the longest and grow the slowest

Sunday food rituals

In the 1960s, shops in vans toured the countryside from house to house selling their wares. Our village in Yorkshire had a little grocery store, and there was also a butcher's van driven by Mr Kirk, who had a shop in Ampleforth village a couple of miles away. During the school holidays we would be eager to go with Mum to the top of the drive and see what was on offer when his van turned up. Fatty lamb shoulder, bacon, minced beef and sausages were the normal fare that Mum would stock up on. Mr Kirk would always give us a slice of polony, pink extruded cured and cooked pork and rusk in a red plastic tube. I loved it! The mince was usually for shepherd's pie or spaghetti bolognaise. I remember the long blue packets of dried spaghetti, which was the only way to buy it at that time. Apart from tinned spaghetti and macaroni cheese, pasta was not a common food until at least a decade later.

The sausage and bacon bought from Mr Kirk would have been for that most special meal of all the week, Sunday breakfast. This was a ritual in our lives that we relished. First you had to earn it by going to church. After this ordeal, we would return home, put a tablecloth on our big table and set the places, ready to indulge in the greatly anticipated treats in store for us. Tinned orange juice and very occasionally tinned grapefruit segments, fried bacon, sausage and eggs. Fresh made white rolls from an overnight dough, usually made by Dad for Sundays only. Homemade marmalade. Our Sunday breakfasts brought a sense of wellbeing and energy to the day.

Sundays had many rituals. Breakfast was followed by being outside – downtime. We were not allowed to be bored. To admit to being bored was always met with

RECIPE

Homemade pork sausage meat

This is as close as I can get to Frank Amis's famous sausage meat I ate as a child. Try to get the very best organic, slow-grown pork. It freezes well for up to three months before it starts to lose flavour.

Ingredients

1 kg pork, coarsely minced
twice by your butcher
2 teaspoons salt
½ teaspoon white pepper.
1 flat dessertspoon dried mixed herbs
(or you can use 2 tablespoons of finely
chopped fresh thyme, rosemary and sage)
½ teaspoon cinnamon
Pinch each of ground cloves and nutmeg

Method

Mix all dry ingredients together well. Sprinkle over the mince and mix well. Leave overnight in the fridge or, if you're freezing the mixture, pack it tightly into a plastic bag (preferably an old one you have washed to reuse), squeezing out any air before freezing.

Shape the mixture into meatballs about the size of a hen's egg, or roll into a sausage shape. Fry in oil gently until nicely browned.

They are simply delicious like this, or you can then add them to a seasonal tomato sauce as part of an Italian pasta dish.

A ritual moment of
gratitude at Lothlorien

Mum saying 'Then go outside and be bored', which of course lead to not being bored. About midday, Dad would go to the pub (or 'on an outing with kids'). Whoever was around would cram into the Mini Traveller and sit outside the Fairfax Arms drinking coke and eating crisps. The entertainment was playing in the brook outside, catching sticklebacks or pretending we could tickle trout.

This pub had one very special offering not to be found in most pubs. Frank Amis the landlord must have kept the odd pig, because every so often Dad would come out of the pub with a big bag of pork sausage meat. Once home, this was usually frozen and then brought out and cooked for Sunday breakfasts as sausage balls. Much later in life I set about learning how to make these using organic pork. In 2017 Better Food won Best Sausage in the Taste of the West Awards with the sausages that are as close as I can get to that memorable flavour.

Perhaps an even more important meal than Sunday breakfast was Sunday supper. This was the Sunday roast with a tablecloth and wine for the grownups. At the table would be all the family and other regulars such as Stephan, who went on to marry our eldest sister Sue. Dad usually cooked, having slept off the lunch-time beer and maybe whisky. We sat around one large table which had to seat 15 or more so it was a tight squeeze for elbows. Dad was a good cook, although tended to only head up the grand meals, due to his school teaching commitments (and the pub visits). There was always lots of hospitality and good cheer and our family Sunday supper instilled in us all a strong sense that sharing meals with friends and family was at the heart of a good life.

Food adventures in the 1960s

My first job in food

At weekends, as a teenager, I worked at the Crown Hotel in Helmsley to earn money, washing up, food prepping, making salads, and then waiting tables.

During my breaks at the Crown I got to eat fantastic food. Sometimes I had the full Sunday roast or even things like Welsh Rarebit. I noted that all the waste from plates and dishes went into the pig bin, which was collected daily by a local pig farmer. The farmer told me he was two-thirds dependent on the hotels and restaurants for his pigs' feed.

Fast food beginnings

My savings from this work enabled me to buy a brand new bike on which I cycled to Nottingham on my own to visit Mary, a family friend who I considered to be my girlfriend. I stopped in Tadcaster at a pub and ordering a half pint and a Ploughman's. I sat outside feeling very grown up and just a little apprehensive that I had not even got a third of the way. Eventually

I got to the outskirts of Nottingham and managed to get on a bus with the bike for the last three miles. The driver was a kind man and helped me pack the bike into the luggage compartment. While staying with the Murtar family I had my first experience of a burger and chips at a Wimpy. At the time, this was beyond a treat. The nearest I'd come to it was the burgers Mum bought from the cash and carry. But I'd never experienced the burger bun before. That soft, sweet, moist bun was the most exciting bit! This fast food soon became a global phenomenon courtesy of Macdonald's. It's a food with no real provenance, and can be eaten without a care for the world. Carolyn Steel explores this issue in her excellent book, *Sitopia*. Ⓡ

Around the same time my brother Mark and I were invited to go to Durham to stay with another family friend, who took us to a brand new motorway service station. It was like something from a sci-fi movie. Hundreds of meals were presented behind what looked like a glass wall. It was full of plates of colourful food in see-through drawers. You chose your meal and put some money in a slot to allow the window of your choice to open. Then you popped this meal into another glass cubicle and it would come out

A spin on cheese on toast

1 medium carrot finely grated
Grated cheese (roughly same weight as carrot)
½ teaspoon of dijon mustard
½ teaspoon miso

Mush all the ingredients to a paste, spread onto a slice of toast and put under a grill for 3 or 4 minutes or until bubbling and changing colour. Eat it with some good brined gherkins or sauerkraut.

Unplug your microwave for a week. See how the minor inconvenience can lead to fun outcomes and more engagement with your food.

Tips

hot in just one minute! The microwave oven had arrived. I have no recollection of what the food was like, only the excitement and the wonder of it all and eating it while looking down on to cars on the motorway.

Microwave ovens

The microwave has become the most universal convenience cooker. I personally have never wanted one or had one in my home. As they go along with little or no involvement with food preparation they lead to food lacking soul.

There are many studies on the use of microwaves. Heating your food in the microwave can strip away its original nutrients. The health benefits of vitamin B-12 are instantly negated once heated in a microwave. The powerful bacteria-fighting agents in breast milk are also destroyed by microwave heating. When you heat foods that are wrapped in plastic in the microwave, you can create carcinogens in the food (Borelli, 2013). ®

Fishing – perch, trout, crayfish and an accidental eel

One weekend, when I was around 12 or 13, my foster brother Davey and I walked a couple of miles across country to some lakes to fish. Davey, at around 15, seemed confident around nature and was an easy companion. There were three lakes belonging to the Ampleforth College estate, some with wild trout, others with pike and perch. We went for the perch, a relatively easy fish to catch. We would put a bit of bread or a worm on the end of a hook and dangle them over the landing stage and watch the fish bite. It was fun but a little too easy, so after a while we pulled up something reminiscent of a lobster pot at the end of a rope in the lake and popped our fish into it, dropping it back in the lake for later collection. It was time to head off to check out the other lakes.

Now we were going for the brown trout. We had no real idea of how to fish and after half an hour or so without a bite or even a sight, we got bored again. And hungry. We had brought no lunch with us. Thankfully, the beck that ran between the lakes was full of crayfish and so we set about catching a load. We found an old pan near a scout hut, washed it out in lake water, made a fire and cooked the crayfish.

The water was a bit earthy and we had no salt or lemon of course, so our meal was super simple. But it was wild food and we were hungry, so they went down very well. We had just finished our feast when one of the monks appeared to reprimand us for trying to fish for trout. You were meant to have a permit for fishing in the lake. Ah well, what did we care?! We grabbed our rods and took off, back to the first lake to pick up our perch. Pulling the rope up, we were amazed to find a huge eel inside the pot along with the perch. This was a heck of a find and of course, had to be killed. How to do it? They are slimy creatures and we had no idea what to do. I am sorry to say we used an oar from a rowing boat and bashed it to death. After much giggling and nervousness, we had our catch in a shoulder bag and were on our way back across the valley fields and home to Oswaldkirk.

Together with the fish, we gave the eel to our neighbours of German descent who were enthusiastic and seemingly had a better idea of what to do with it. Later in life on a holiday in Eastern Germany I discovered the true delights of eating wild eel both fresh and smoked.

We found an old pan, washed it out in lake water, made a fire and cooked the crayfish

Food as sanctuary

As a teenager, food, both cultivated and wild, offered me some sanctuary from the craziness of family life, which was causing me much unhappiness. I found that when I worked with food in any way, I felt a little safer, a little stronger. It was something to hold on to. Eating our own eggs from my chickens, our own veg from Mum's garden, home cooked bread, various wild foods from mushrooms to sorrel to blackberries and apples, formed a kind of important and stabilising structure for me.

A hare

One of my dad's drinking haunts was a place called The Star at Harem. There were always gamekeepers (or maybe poachers) in the pub and one day not only did Dad appear with the usual brace of pheasants, but also a large hare. After a few days of hanging, it was time to skin and gut it. I was the oldest in the house that evening. Although I'd never skinned anything before, I had seen it done with rabbits. I set to and was getting on very well, or so I thought. Engrossed in my work, I managed to cut my index finger. The cut was so deep that it severed the tendons, causing lasting damage. Once some help arrived, the hare was done and ready to cook. We ate hare casserole around the huge kitchen table, while I bathed in the attention to my bandaged finger that would never again, to this day, be straight. Hares are no longer in abundance and so seldom is it allowed or wise to take one for the pot. This is a direct consequence of our farming methods. I have no doubt that when we return (and return we must) to better farming practice, hares will thrive again in the English countryside and we will be able to enjoy this delicious wild meat once more.

A brief pause to indulge

Take a bottle of organic, French red table wine. Open it, smell it and think about the grapes that made it ripening in the sunshine and warmth of southern France. Take some good (preferably unpasteurised) cheese. Leave both cheese and wine to relax and come to room temperature. Add a few oat cakes, not just any oat cake but the very best (I love the Village Bakery ones, although I rarely find them anymore). Tuck in. As your mouth delights in the tastes, textures and aromas, with glass in hand close your eyes and imagine you are somewhere that has made any of these products. Perhaps you can even visualise yourself as one of the makers for a moment. Bask in the glory of these gifts of nature combined with the hands of people who care deeply about the food they make.

Supermarkets

Throughout the 1980s and 90s I beat the drum for local, organic food. My thinking and passions developed from my time working on the land and learning about organic farming into wanting to make my mark on growing the market for organic food, locally sourced. I wanted to connect more growers with a local market and help my customers understand the importance of the health of our soils, our animals and indeed humanity's reliance on this for its own health..

Supermarkets are a conglomerate approach to food distribution that came about to exploit a revolution in choice, processing options and packaging. Their rise went alongside a huge increase in the number of households where both adults were in work. As a result, shopping became a planned weekly excursion with the convenience of everything being under one roof. It was exciting for people to be exposed, often for the first time, to a huge range of foods to try. It was part of an aspiring, progressive time where these places felt like progress and made us feel rich.

Sadly, no one stopped to question the impact of this grocery revolution. Supermarkets have little or no interest in health, quality of life or wellbeing. They ruthlessly and cynically exploit farmers, processors and of course consumers to ensure the highest returns to shareholders. It's almost universally a terrible system that, at best, provides a volume of food to the masses. At worst, supermarkets destroy farming livelihoods and communities, plunder the earth's resources and deliver ill health both nutritionally as well as psychologically through poor quality food to a dumbed down population. (Renton, A, 2011 and Bland, A, 2014) Ⓡ

It is this that motivated me to do more about creating a business in organic, local and ethical retailing.

But (I hear you say) supermarkets are both efficient and cheaper!

Yes, but at what cost? Cheaper food does not mean a cheaper life. The current system of food production required by the supermarkets is costing the earth and we have only one planet available to exploit. Actually, there is only one way forward for food and farming. A system that pays full attention to nature first, then people and profit last. We will all discover this at some point in the future of humanity and when we do, I hope the discovery will lead to repairing culture and rebuilding communities fit for a new world. In fact we are finding this out right now. As I write, Covid-19 is bringing the world to its knees and is exposing the huge lack of resilience in our food system. Who is going to plant and pick if we can't exploit migrant workers? Where is our food security if imports dry up due to lack of planting, harvesting and transport? Just eight weeks after Covid-19 emerged in the UK, fresh produce imports started to climb in price and availability began to decrease.

66
The current system of food production is costing the earth

Realistically, some people have more money than others. Some of us who read about such matters and who care about the provenance of their food are able to afford to buy as they choose. Many, understandably, have other priorities. Let's be generous with ourselves. Use the supermarkets when we need to, choosing local and seasonal if available, and seek local and organic retailers when possible. It is not in our interests to feel bad or guilty about the choices we make. Rather we can celebrate heartily when we do find ways to better connect with our food and nature.

These days we are used to lots of choice. The media is crammed with mouthwatering dishes and recipes that encourage us to buy from the huge range of ingredients that are available to satiate our desires. Perhaps if there was less choice and more 'pick of the day', 'catch of the day' or 'dish of the day', we could

simply celebrate what is, rather than feeling the necessity to always have a specific ingredient. This is a sort of gluttony that also leads us to enjoying our food less. We can probably all recall a time when we were really hungry and we ate something simple that tasted sublime. This is the joy that food can offer and the less hungry we are when we eat, the less we tend to enjoy it. Buying a vegetable box made up of produce that the farmer most needs to harvest can help bring back some surprise and adventure to our cooking and eating.

Let's seek ways to find some self-confidence in the preparation of food that will serve us well in life as well as in health. It's a journey filled with variety and fun – just a little bit of effort can offer wonderful outcomes.

Walled gardens and café

In 2002, we took on Barley Wood Walled Gardens near Wrington in North Somerset. These superb Victorian gardens with a café in part of an old tool store and workshops, covered about an acre. High walls supported mature espalier fruit trees. There were fabulous box hedges with big herbaceous borders and four sections of vegetables. The gardens were on a gentle south-facing slope with an old brick path looking up to the Mendip Hills. This was the real deal, a Victorian style garden to feed the big house.

It was a joy and a privilege to have this chance to work on such old and well-restored gardens. As a keen plantswoman, my wife Gerry worked on the herbaceous borders and I managed the gardens with help from various gardeners. There were many Saturday mornings when having harvested since dawn, on occasions with head torch, I would take the produce to our shop for about 9 am. People would soon gather to eye the glistening fresh organic greens, fabulous small stem asparagus, bunch carrots, bunch beetroots, onions and the superb soft fruit in July and August. It all caused a buzz and an excitement in St Werburghs as if a farmers' market had just opened for the first time.

This was the real deal, a Victorian style garden to feed the big house

Barley Wood overlooking the Mendip Hills

Quiche or tart

When I ran the walled garden this was our staple lunch offer, served with garden salad. We made the quiches in batches of three or four and always used shallow tin bases with removable bottoms, which were much better for blind baking the pastry. We were clear about one thing. We wanted an unctuous tart made with organic butter, eggs and cream.

Pastry for 23 cm quiche tin

125 g very cold butter
250 g plain white flour
(Use wholemeal if you like
– it's very different but just
as good and more nutritious.)
A little very cold water
Salt

Custard mix

4 eggs
125 ml double cream
200 ml milk
½ teaspoon salt
Pepper to taste

Filling options

There are so many to choose from. Use a seasonal veg, or anything left over in the fridge will do. At the gardens we used all the small asparagus spears, also courgette, spinach and even sweetcorn taken off the cob when these were small or not well filled out. We sometimes used cheese, but again the recipe is good for using up pieces that were on the tired side.

Method

To make the pastry, tip the flour and butter into a bowl, then rub together with your fingertips until completely mixed and crumbly. Add 8 tablespoons of cold water, then bring everything together with your hands until just combined. Roll into a ball and use straight away or chill for up to two days. You can do the first part of this in a food processor or mixer on pulse only, but do it gently and always finish it with your hands.

Roll out and place in your greased tin or dish. Allow it to flow over the edge a little. Cut this back to just over the edge, and blind bake with parchment and beans for 15 to 20 minutes at 180 deg C.

While it's in the oven, prepare your custard. Whisk all ingredients together with seasoning.

Turn the oven down to about 160 deg C. Now if there are signs of any cracking in your pastry, get a pastry brush and brush some of your custard mix into the cracks while still very hot. Five minutes or so after you've removed the case from the oven trim the edges again with a knife if necessary.

Add your filling to the pastry case. Then take your dish to the oven pull out a shelf to place it on. Gently pour your jug of custard mix into the case. Fill it to as close to the top of the case as possible, without it spilling in your oven. I push the tray back into the oven a little way when it's half full so that it feels more stable while I add the rest. You could also place a bigger oven dish in the bottom of the oven to catch any drip or spills.

Bake for 30 to 40 minutes. You want it lightly brown on top, but you do not want to over cook. It's much nicer to have a tiny bit of ooze than to have a rubbery texture.

Enjoy this with a selection of garden salad if possible. Maybe, if you feel like it, think about how this delicious nutritious meal has come to you. The people, the cows, the chickens and the soils of our generous Earth.

Cooking with friends

My sister, Liz

Cooking with family and friends is something all my siblings are very at home with, and my sister Liz in particular does it effortlessly. Liz is a natural around food and conviviality and has a great eye for design and creating homely places. Liz made her mark on the Bristol café food scene when she took on The Folk House in 2012. Buying organic vegetables from our wholesale department she served up simple delicious dishes and cakes. It was another Haughton food place that sparkled with love, care, conviviality and ethics.

Inspired by some of my time in those walled gardens and other places, here is a challenge for a fabulous meal for friends to share, both in the preparation as well as the eating. Allow time!

Gather family and or friends in the kitchen. Start a conversation about food and what you have available to you right now. Maybe you need to go to a shop, or the allotment, or just the fridge. Give some thought to the season, the weather, your need for warmth or coolness. Trust that you can cook a good meal together, without referring to any recipe.

Take all your gathered ingredients and lay them out, without making any decisions about what you will do with them – yet. Look at them, handle them, smell the produce. Take it in turns to talk about things you have done with some of these ingredients in the past.

Now it's decision time. Sometimes I have to begin to prep the vegetables before I know what I am actually going to do. Start to cook, all the while being conscious of the food, where it comes from and what it might taste like. Stay as flexible as you feel able to be. You might change your mind halfway through and add a tin of beans, or do some noodles with it. Perhaps the smell of the cooking might make you realise you want some other ingredient added at some point. Cheese, or bacon, or miso, or wine, or fresh herbs, or lemon zest. It could be any manner of things. Pause before adding any additional ingredients, but trust your senses to know what will work.

Sharing this experience with friends and family can really help our confidence and ability to cook without recipes. It's great to cook with others, bouncing ideas off each other. When you all get to sit down to eat, try to have a conversation about what you have cooked and what it was like for you cooking without a recipe or even an idea of what you might cook.

Seasonality

Taking on the walled gardens brought me even closer to the seasons. Over the past 40 years two major things have changed our eating habits. Firstly, supermarkets began to offer us more out-of-season foods. Now we can have strawberries, asparagus, mangetout or whatever we want all the year around shipped from all over the world. Secondly, we have found ways of growing food on a commercial scale that stretches the seasons within our own UK climate by the use of controlled environments in growing and storage. We would do well to cut out much of the out-of-season imports and celebrate the short season produce more when it is naturally growing in our climate. Let's import citrus from Europe because we can't grow it here and go back to being extremely good apple growers in the UK, knowing we may well not eat a single apple between March and August.

Extending our own seasons using greenhouses and polytunnels as well the use of hybrid seed varieties makes sense to me and as a grower it helps commercially to spread income over more of the year. For me the most important thing is to celebrate our fresh produce and enjoy the food that is grown as near to home as possible during its natural season.

Apples

Ever since my Real Food Supplies days I have been blessed to know the Pardoe family of apple growers from Herefordshire. In 1986, Ian Pardoe walked into the shop on Gloucester Road dressed in his biker jacket (I later heard he was regularly to be found at big biker gatherings). We have been buying apples from him and his son Joe ever since. Joe has kept the family business growing since Ian died. In 2016 I called Joe about doing some apple juice for us at Better Food. Joe is so passionate and energetic, he wanted to help make this happen and was happy to sell us grade out apples for juicing. He knew every variety and where it was in his apple store and when it could be accessed. We organised the apples to be brought to Barley Wood orchard where a lovely couple, Isi and Mike, have set up a business making cider from the orchard apples. They were happy to press Joe's apples for us in their big old cider press. The press sits within a wonderful cedar shingle round house built by Ian Hillman. It was a real pleasure to be invited to watch a pressing as they wound the great handle applying tons to the pressure on the apples with juice pouring out into vats ready to bottle, pasteurise, and label for our shops.

The juice from Joe's apples has become a staple own brand in Better Food stores. It is much loved by our customers for its simplicity and provenance, not to mention superb flavour. Thank you, Joe. Great juice. And thank you too for the wonderful supply of apples, pears, plums and cherries that you have grown for over 30 years.

The hungry gap

The hungry gap is the time when all winter crops have come to an end and all we have are stored roots and a few hardy leeks in the ground. April and May are busy times for growers as they sow the crops for later in the year. At this time they are harvesting just small amounts of spring crops.

In the walled garden during the hungry gap we would have lots of winter cabbages that had been

Let's celebrate our fresh produce and enjoy the food that's grown as near to home as possible during its natural season

Asparagus – a treat
for the hungry gap

with an orchard in the grounds, we were able to use apples, pears, plums and soft fruit in many of our cakes and puddings. Sunday lunches were always packed out and I learned to be a café chef cooking up to 60 organic roast dinners as well as the more standard café fare. In 2006 we won *The Guardian* Café of the Year Award. As we got even busier, my son Charlie helped at weekends, getting his first taste of the catering world.

It was a privilege to be custodian of this beautiful place for a few years and to witness the delight of our customers as they ate the produce they could see growing while looking out of the café window.

There were two crops in particular that I grew to love during my time at Barley Wood.

cut leaving just the stumps. The winter salads were almost over, but all these would put out shoots and go to flower within a few weeks of the warming weather in April.

Just before it's time to plant other vegetables in their place you can pick sprouting greens of various colours, sizes and flavours. These are similar to purple sprouting broccoli and they all make great stir fry material, or are delicious simply steamed. If you have an allotment or a vegetable patch, leave these greens in until they sprout. Or, if you're not a grower, ask for them in your shop, or from your box scheme.

Barley Wood Café

A year after we took on the gardens we took over the walled garden café as well. We made some changes to the food offer and started to focus on what was growing in the gardens. Seasonal salads and vegetables were served with simple quiches (see recipe on page 59), pasties and café-type foods. Of course, being a tea room, cakes were important and

Asparagus

The asparagus beds down at the bottom of the gardens were mature and abundant. On hot days in June the crop would grow so fast you would have to pick twice a day. The beds had been set up so well by Ian Hillman and we were the lucky benefactors of his labour. To cook and eat asparagus within two hours of picking is one of the greatest and simplest of joys. In May and June asparagus would appear as a daily special - blanched, buttered and drizzled with lemon juice. Full stop. We also chargrilled the stems and served them as a salad with baby leaves from the garden and shavings of parmesan.

Perhaps the best way of all of eating asparagus is while you're cutting it. Straight in the mouth, crunch, and that exquisite pea-like flavour so fresh, so unique. Can't beat it as a perk of the picker.

Fig and garden grape jam with wine

I am very fortunate to have a fig tree, which I don't get many figs from, unlike the trees at the Walled Garden. However, I do get enough small and damaged ones to use for jam. I also have a grapevine that is useless for eating, but has big bunches of very small grapes with lots of flavour. This preserve brings those two ingredients together to great effect.

Ingredients

500 g or so of grapes
500 g fresh figs chopped
150 ml of wine, red if grapes
are red, white if grapes are white

Method

Boil up the grapes and wine for about 15 minutes.

Push the mixture through a sieve to produce a grape juice. Discard the skin and pips. Add the chopped figs to the juice. You can even use good quality dried figs for this, but if you do soak them in water for a few hours first.

You will have around 200 ml of liquid and to this you need to add the juice of a lemon and about 250 g sugar. Bring to the boil and then boil and stir for about 10 minutes before testing on a plate. It will not set fully, but will have a syrupy jam consistency when cool.

Ready to press apples with
Joe Pardoe and Mike Atkins

Figs

There was a fig tree just inside the main public entrance growing against a big 10-foot wall. These walls acted as fantastic night storage heaters soaking up daytime sun and releasing the heat during the night. Picking ripe figs off any tree in Europe is a delight, but to do so in the UK is even more special.

The figs were at times prolific and at the end of the season there were many small ones from which I made jam combined with great bunches of small, pippy, slightly sour grapes. It's a jam that needs some booze added to it and it's delicious.

I am now growing both asparagus and figs in our garden at home and, while not set in those perfect conditions, they are a delight worth waiting for. The brief season of both elevates them to culinary joy.

Growing, harvesting and storing borlotti beans

I adore fresh borlotti beans. For the past five years I've been growing them at home and now would never not grow them.

Growing borlotti beans

You can raise plants from seed under heat in March or April. I start mine early because I can offer them some outdoor protection when they go out in early May. Once chilly winds and all frosts have gone, it's safe to put plants out without any fleece or such like. Of course, you can simply plant the seeds in May, but having tried both ways I found I had better results bringing on plug plants.

The ground should be well cultivated and fertile. Beans prefer a slightly acid soil, but don't worry too much about that, just make sure it's free draining. A sunny spot is best. You can add the bean poles after planting, but whether you make a row or a wigwam, make sure the beans are tucked just inside the cane to avoid damage. I give mine two feeds of seaweed liquid manure over the summer and keep weeding regularly.

Start to harvest around the end of August or early Sept when the first pods are plump and the beans are turning speckled pink. If they are green, they are under ripe.

Keep picking as you need them and then leave the bulk to ripen until the pods start to go darker and the bean walls start to thin as the energy is transferred to the bean and it starts to mature. The beans will dry a fair bit on the plant if its not rainy, but ripe beans will start to mould if the weather is too wet. Pod and dry them on trays before putting them in jars in the store cupboard. Very pleasing!

Eating borlotti beans

An end-of-summer salad with fresh borlotti beans is like heaven. Get creative with them and use whatever else you have in the garden to complement them.

When the evenings start to draw in and you want a warming supper these beans make fabulous casseroles. It's great to cook them in vegetable or chicken stock and I like lots of ground coriander with them. If you grow coriander, you'll find it often goes to seed so, for the best flavour, grab a fistful of green seed and mash it up to add to the casserole. Carrots, garlic and onion are the staples of a good casserole helping to lend it a rounded, sweet flavour.

Here's a very quick recipe, but have a play and add to it what you like.

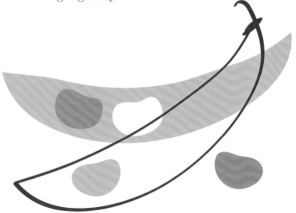

Borlotti bean casserole

Ingredients

About 1.2 kg fresh borlotti beans, shelled (600 g shelled weight)
100 ml extra virgin olive oil, plus extra for drizzling
2 onions, sliced
3 garlic cloves chopped
Good pinch chilli flakes (optional)
Small bunch fresh sage leaves, half left whole, half roughly chopped
600 g vine tomatoes, roughly chopped
Pinch sugar (optional)
200–300 ml vegetable stock
Small bunch fresh oregano leaves, roughly chopped

Method

Put the shelled beans in a large pan of water. Bring to the boil, then turn down the heat and simmer for 15–30 minutes or until tender. The time they take can vary quite a bit. Drain and set aside.

Heat the oil in a heavy pan and fry the onions gently until soft but not coloured. Add garlic and chilli flakes plus whole sage leaves, then cook for a few minutes more. Add the tomatoes. Bring to a simmer, stirring until reduced a little, maybe 7 or 8 minutes. Add the borlottis and 200 ml stock and bring to a gentle simmer, then cook for another 8–10 minutes until the beans are just beginning to fall apart.

Serve, pouring a little olive oil over each dish and scattering with the remaining herbs.

Charlie Haughton

Charlie is a cook, bread maker and occasional vegetable grower, and co-creator of Pitchfork Café, which hosts seasonal, vegan fundraising meals in Bristol; he is interested in addressing the social and political issues around food and eating.

Our food system in this country is broken. That much is sure. Supermarkets have driven down prices and more than ever people expect to find cheap food on the shelves. The food people are consuming is nutritionally void and the farming techniques that we are reliant on for feeding us are depleting the soil and damaging the environment.

Whilst it is easy to lay blame on supermarkets or conventional farming, that accusation falls short of recognising them both as symptoms of the capitalist system they are working within. It is capitalism that leaves millions of people without access to food whilst crops rot in the ground, and it is capitalism that forces small-scale farmers that are reliant on a cut-throat market to intensify production or go bust. It is capitalism that replaces rainforests with monocrop farms and capitalism that causes antibiotic overuse. The list goes on...

This is not to say that the only way we can improve access to food is to overthrow capitalism (although

we should always have that in mind). Alternative models can exist within our society. These models should go beyond mimicking existing 'successful' food businesses and acknowledge that there are financial and social barriers that prevent large groups of the population from accessing well-produced and nutritious food. Until these barriers are acknowledged and acted upon then sustainable alternatives will be exclusive to a privileged minority.

It is a big ask for the small businesses that provide good quality food to also address social problems. Most farmers work unsustainable hours already and the majority of small food businesses operate on a financial knife edge. We need to look away from business as usual and focus on models that are centred on community involvement and ownership. Models that empower people from all parts of society to be growing, cooking and eating good quality food. We should learn from ideas such as community supported agriculture (CSA) and replicate them across all parts of the food chain. The food supply chain should be shrunk down wherever possible and waste will inevitably be reduced in the process – although on a side note, whilst that food waste still exists let us reclaim it, distribute it to our communities and feast on its bountiful hoards!

It is obvious that we can't wait around for agri-businesses and supermarkets to wake up and realise the damage they are doing, nor will the state suddenly turn around and fix food insecurity issues or reverse environmental degradation. It is up to us to build long-term political movements that address the root causes of these problems and create sustainable alternatives that provide nutritious and well-produced food for all.

The food supply chain should be shrunk down wherever possible

Celeriac croquettes

Makes approximately 20 croquettes

Ingredients

1 large celeriac
½ onion, roughly chopped
Bay leaves and thyme
600 ml soy milk
4 heaped tablespoons plain flour
3 heaped tablespoons margarine
Approx 200 g breadcrumbs
(preferably panko)
1 tablespoon each of dijon and
wholegrain mustard

Method

Peel celeriac and cut half of it into roughly 2.5 cm sized pieces. Put in a medium-sized pan with the onion, thyme and bay, salt and pepper and pour in the soy milk to cover the celeriac. Cut a circular piece of greaseproof paper to put in the pan to stop too much liquid evaporating. Cook on a medium heat for 25–30 minutes, or until really soft. Meanwhile, dice the other half of the celeriac into 2 cm pieces and roast in the oven with salt and oil at 160 C for 30–40 minutes. Now whizz it in a food processor to make a rough textured paste. Strain the milk and celeriac mixture through a sieve, pushing it with the back of a spoon to get maximum liquid. Keep the liquid in a jug and discard the pulp.

Next make a bechamel sauce. Check that you have 350 ml of the celeriac milk, if not then add a bit more. Put the margarine into a small pan and melt then add the plain flour and mix together to a smooth thick paste with a wooden spoon. Cook out for 2–3 minutes then add the celeriac milk gradually, mixing with vigour all the time with a wooden spoon to incorporate without lumps. When all the milk has been added you should be left with a sauce that is thicker than your average bechamel, but still smooth and creamy. If it's too runny then this will make it more difficult later so sieve a bit of plain flour into it and whisk it in and cook out for a few minutes. Now add the whizzed up roast celeriac plus the dijon and wholegrain mustards and a pinch of cracked black pepper. Mix thoroughly and then taste for seasoning. Pour the mix into a bowl or tray and place a piece of greaseproof paper over the surface to stop a skin forming. Leave in the fridge to cool completely.

Take the mix out of the fridge and set up a breadcrumbing station. Place next to each other a plate with plain flour on, a bowl of soy milk and another wider plate with breadcrumbs. Prepare to get messy! This process is quite involved and can be tricky at first but it will get easier. Be as careful as you can when handling the mix. Use two spoons to shape the celeriac mix (Google how to make a quenelle!). You want the outsides to be smooth if possible but don't worry too much about the shape. Let the quenelled mix fall off the spoon onto the floured plate and gently roll it in flour. Pick it up as delicately as you can and roll it in your palm to get rid of excess flour then drop it in the bowl of soy milk and sloosh it about so it gets covered in milk. Pick it up and then drop it onto the plate of breadcrumbs, roll it until it is well coated then place it on a tray lined with greaseproof paper. Repeat the process until all the mix is done. Store in the fridge if you're not going to cook immediately.

Either deep-fry or shallow-fry in 2 cm oil in a frying pan until the croquettes are golden brown all over. Drain them on some kitchen paper on a plate and leave to cool for a couple of minutes before eating. They can be hotter than the sun!

Resources
Better cook and eat

Organisations for better cooking and eating

Square Food Foundation, Bristol
www.squarefoodfoundation.co.uk

Sustainable Food Trust
sustainablefoodtrust.org

Green America
www.greenamerica.org

Books

Steel, Carolyn (2020) *Sitopia: How food can save the world*, Chatto & Windus.

Tree, Isabella (2019) *Wilding: The return of nature to a British farm*, Picador.

Wright, John (2007) *Mushrooms (River Cottage Handbook No1)*, Bloomsbury.

Wright, John (2009) *Edible Seashore (River Cottage Handbook no 5)*, Bloomsbury.

Wright, John (2010) *Hedgerow (River Cottage Handbook no 7)*, Bloomsbury.

Articles, blogs, web

Bland, A (2014) 'Supermarkets care nothing for our health. That's our job', Independent, 15 June, www.independent.co.uk/life-style/health-and-families/health-news/supermarkets-care-nothing-for-our-health-thats-our-job-9537729.html (accessed 9 June 2020)

Borelli, L (2013) 'Microwaves Are Bad For You: 5 Reasons Why Microwave Oven Cooking Is Harming Your Health', *Medical Daily* www.medicaldaily.com/microwaves-are-bad-you-5-reasons-why-microwave-oven-cooking-harming-your-health-250145 (accessed 25 May 2020

Castelow, Ellen 'Food in Britain in the 1950s and 1960s', *Historic UK*, www.historic-uk.com/CultureUK/Food-in-Britain-in-the-1950s-1960s/ (accessed 9 June 2020)

Green America, 'Food and climate', https://www.greenamerica.org/food-climate (accessed 12 June 2020)

Knicky, M & Spörndly R (2009) 'Sodium benzoate, potassium sorbate and sodium nitrate as silage additives', *Journal of the Science of Food and Agriculture*, www.researchgate.net/publication/229447035_Sodium_benzoate_potassium_sorbate_and_sodium_nitrite_as_silage_additives (accessed 25 May 2020)

Miers, Thomasina (2013) 'Let pigs eat swill and stop wasting precious resources', *The Guardian*, 23 November, www.theguardian.com/commentisfree/2013/nov/23/food-waste-recycling-pigs-farming (accessed 9 June 2020)

Renton, A (2011) 'British farmers forced to pay the cost of supermarket price wars', *The Guardia*n, 2 July, https://www.independent.co.uk/life-style/health-and-families/health-news/supermarkets-care-nothing-for-our-health-thats-our-job-9537729.html (accessed 25 May 2020)

The Royal Society (2001) 'The role of land carbon sinks in mitigating world climate change', royalsociety.org/-/media/Royal_Society_Content/policy/publications/2001/9996.pdf

Young, Richard (2014) 'What meat to eat?', sustainablefoodtrust.org/articles/the-meat-debate-red-meat/ (accessed 9 June 2020)

> The greatest action we can all take to mend our food system is to grow our own food

Better farm and grow

Changing our ways for the sake of soil and human health

Our food system has failed us and yet it would be actually one of the easiest things to change, were it not for the global companies dominating our food and farming systems. From seed to table, the conglomerate capitalist machine has become ever more efficient at monopolising and exploiting our food for profit. As a system this no longer supports our health, our families, our communities and certainly not our soils and our animals.

However, there are so many wonderful projects growing food, sharing with and benefiting many others who want a change in our food system. These projects are the beating heart of a better way to grow and offer opportunities for everyone to learn more about how we can feed ourselves in a manner that is sustainable for the planet. They show us the way.

And the good news is that as much as 60% of the food produced in the world is still produced by small-scale or subsistence farmers. Now is the time to ask all farmers to produce food for our communities using good sustainable methods that are in harmony with nature. We need to stop talking as if every farmer should be trying to feed the world. This is a big shift, but empowers communities and encourages localism. The planet will feed us if we take care of it and respect it and all it has to offer.

Phil talked to...
Jackie and Alan Gear

In 1973 Alan and Jackie Gear went to work for the Henry Doubleday Research Association (now Garden Organic). They were appointed joint directors in 1986 and stayed until 2003, during which time it grew to become the largest organic growing organisation in Europe. They have written and broadcast widely on organic food, farming and gardening and have received MBEs for services to organic horticulture research.

Phil: What's important to you about organic gardening and growing?

Alan and Jackie: As scientists in the early 1970s, after hearing the conclusions of the 1972 UN Conference on the Environment at Stockholm, we decided to change careers and go to work for HDRA, a small organic horticultural charity. We did this because we recognised that the environment and wildlife were being seriously harmed by the chemicals and practices then being used by farmers and gardeners.

Organic gardening and growing methods, on the other hand, were known to be sustainable, improve soil fertility naturally, encourage a rich diversity of wildlife and avoid the use of potentially harmful chemicals. Also, organic cultivation has worldwide relevance and is universally practical.

What's more, we now know that organic food contains more vitamins, minerals and phytochemicals, which help to maintain us in good health. And it tastes better too!

We decided to make research into organic gardening, commercial horticulture and food our life's work.

Phil: Do you have any suggestions for people as to how they can do/act/work to make change in the world around farming and growing?

Jackie: All of us these days can help our planet by going organic. We can source food as locally as possible to save food miles. Growing your own is the best – even if you only have a balcony you can raise a couple of tomato plants, herbs and salad plants. Or you can get an allotment, perhaps share a neighbour's garden, or become involved with a Community Supported Agriculture (CSA) scheme. In some towns, people are even cultivating derelict sites, roadside verges and unused patches of land, like the inspiring Incredible Edible Todmorden project. When buying food we can choose local, specialist shops or sign up to a vegetable box scheme.

Joining organisations like the Soil Association, Garden Organic and the Sustainable Food Trust, which campaign for greener growing, is a great way to help change the world for the better.

Public events like Apple and Potato Days, Chilli Fiestas, and local vegetable seed swaps all help to keep alive our rich diversity of fruit and vegetable varieties – and they're fun!

Phil: What do our leaders and governors need to do most to help make change?

Alan: We can lobby our leaders to make changes that will encourage and enable us all to eat organic food and stop the damage being done to the environment by modern intensive agriculture, with its destruction of habitats and contribution to global warming and pesticide pollution. The government should direct agricultural support payments towards environmentally sustainable organic producers.

The government needs to educate society across the board about the dangers of eating junk food. Diseases like cancer, obesity and diabetes are financially crippling the NHS. It should advise people to eat a locally sourced, organic wholefood diet.

A national drive to make more allotments available to people living in urban areas, like the wartime Dig for Victory campaign, could make a significant contribution to improving food security and health and well-being.

Parsnip and apple soup

This delicious seasonal soup, combining the sweetness of my favourite vegetable, the parsnip, with the balancing sharpness of a cooking apple is great during the colder months. Use fresh ingredients if you possibly can.

Ingredients

2 large parsnips
1 large onion
1 large cooking apple
25 g unsalted butter
600 ml vegetable stock
½ teaspoon dried mixed herbs
600 ml milk
sea salt and black pepper to taste
2 tablespoons chopped fresh parsley

Serves 4

Scrub the parsnips, peel the onion and remove the core from the apple. Chop into evenly sized pieces. Melt the butter in a large saucepan and add the vegetables and fruit. Stir well and cook until the onion is transparent. Add the vegetable stock and the dried mixed herbs, bring to the boil then reduce the heat and simmer with the lid on for 30 minutes.

Remove from the heat and add the milk. Leave to cool slightly then blend in a liquidiser. Return to the pan, add salt and pepper to taste and reheat. At the last moment add freshly chopped parsley and serve.

Early years gardening and the homestead food production

Growing vegetables at Manor Field

In 1964 we moved to a village called Oswaldkirk in Yorkshire. Our new home, Manor Field, was a brand new bungalow, purpose built for our very large family. The house was designed with a big kitchen at its heart. It had an Aga of course and a far-from-ordinary table. Made by Mr Yeoman for the family it had a plain Formica top, was about 9 feet long and incredibly strong and sturdy. The table is still in use to this day in the Lothlorien community (see page 105).

Manor Field was set in a huge garden, big enough for Mum to plant an orchard, a vegetable patch and a rose bed, and still have plenty of room for play areas, sheds and more. Mum marked out for us children our own little growing beds that we planted with annual flowers and radishes. I expect they got very weedy and lay abandoned after a few months but it was a valuable introduction to what happens to seeds when you sow and water them. By the time I was about 10 I was helping Mum in the garden with the vegetable patch, which took up a fair bit of her time. I was the ideal candidate. I enjoyed pleasing Mum, so planting potatoes or digging out carrots or leeks became one of my jobs.

One year when the whole garden had got out of hand because Mum had been on a lecture tour in the US, we had a big family garden day to help get it back under control. There was plenty of weeding, mowing, chopping and burning done with Dad allocating tasks to suit our ages and capabilities. At the end of the day Dad took all the older ones to the pub to eat. I was really chuffed because I was allowed to go. I was growing up! Mum was producing significant amounts of vegetables from our garden, and my part in its production helped me build confidence around soil and plants.

Left: The family at the table
Right: Mum gardening

Keeping chickens

By the time I was 14 I had been keeping chickens for some time. They provided delicious eggs for the whole family to enjoy. I got great satisfaction from being responsible for feeding and caring for these birds and supplying the family. I read up on how to increase daylight length with electric lights so they laid eggs later into the season. I had two breeds, Rhode Island Reds and White Leghorns. Both were traditional egg laying breeds. However, these were already being largely replaced on farms by highly commercial breeds that started laying earlier at 16 weeks old and then kept on laying eggs every day until they were 72 weeks old, when they would be culled. My birds laid less than half this quantity of eggs for about eight months of the year. Naturally, hens stop laying to go into a period of moult, when they shed feathers and regrow new ones. This takes all the energy that would have gone into laying. My birds went on laying each year, although a little less each year that passed. When they were about three years old or more we would eat them, giving them a long slow cook to make a hearty nutritious broth or stew.

Commercial egg laying chicken farms have in excess of 4000 birds and often up to 30,000 in one unit. These birds have little access to outdoors even when in full lay, and even if they are 'free range'.

A really good organic free-range unit will have no more than 2000 hens, all of which have daily access to outdoors from an early age. (See Soil Association in resources.) Ⓡ

You can easily keep your own chickens – see the resources for more information. When it comes to feeding your birds, I encourage you to think about what you want to eat yourself and how the feed is produced. Organic feed helps protect birds, bees and biodiversity in a way that chemical feeds cannot claim to do. Ⓡ

1930s threshing machine

The farm next door

Manor Farm was in its last years of active agricultural productivity as a farm unit. It later became a housing estate. The farm had several old stone outbuildings and no farmhouse.

The autumn of 1965 was the one and only time I have seen the threshing of wheat sheaves. It took place below the farm buildings. There was a huge stack of sheaves, maybe 12 feet high and as long as a big farm trailer. These would have been cut from a local field, which in those days would have had a fair amount of weeds, poppies and the like, all helping to support bird life and biodiversity. On the sunny morning in question a huge machine turned up. This machine would have been hired and taken from farm to farm threshing the corn. It was in two parts - the thresher and a tractor - with massive belts to transfer the tractor power to the thresher.

Men climbed the stack with a ladder and pitchforked sheaves onto the thresher, which then divided the wheat from the chaff. Slowly, over many hours, the stack went down with one man forking the threshed straw away onto another big pile. This was great for jumping into, which of course earned us a thick ear from the farmer.

The wheat flowed slowly into huge hessian sacks and was then put on a trailer. These sacks could weigh over 180 lbs (80 kg) and yet one man would be expected to lift them onto the trailer on his own. This was farm life and it wasn't until the late 1960s or early 70s that farm labourers got any real rights with regard to lifting heavy sacks.

Here is a clip from a union document objecting to the Ministry's lack of concern for farm labourers' welfare.

It is not good enough in 1960, for the Ministry to tell farm workers that they must lift any weight their bosses tell them to lift until 1965, when the new proposals will become operative, when they will not be forced to carry more than 180 lbs (over 80 kg), and at about the same time another Ministry, the Ministry of Labour, has issued a pamphlet entitled, "Lifting and Carrying", under the No. I new series of the Safety, Health and Welfare Regulations, recommending that the maximum load for lifting in industry should be 130 lbs (60 kg).

I'm not sure that today any of us could even begin to understand how to go about lifting weights over 50 kg, never mind 80 kg! A farm labourer's life in the 1960s was very tough, with hernias being commonplace, unsurprisingly.

The wheat that came from this threshing would have been kibbled and fed to livestock. I doubt it would have made good bread. Bread wheat needs a high gluten content and our climate is not the best for this. While in a good summer we may well produce bread wheat, some of which will be used by manufacturers for biscuit and pastry flour, the bulk goes to feed livestock.

Men climbed the stack with a ladder and pitchforked sheaves onto the thresher

Dairy farming

The dairy industry

When I was a small child, we lived next to a dairy farm which provided us with delicious and very fresh milk every day. Sounds great doesn't it? However, the farm was part of a 2000-acre estate owned by Ampleforth College, which had a strong eye on bottom line profit and saw the latest technology and agrichemical solutions as necessary. It used the latest chemicals recommended to deal with growing issues around pests and disease, which stemmed from the overuse of chemical fertilisers. By the end of February each year, some of the barns that had been filled with hay and straw now contained hundreds of fertiliser sacks. This was in the days when DDT was still in use and the chemical companies were offering miracles and making millions. Common Market subsidies were also about to produce one food mountain after another, including huge 'milk lakes'. As late as 2003, it was reported that the EU warehoused 194,000 tonnes of powdered milk and 223,000 tonnes of butter. (BBC, 2016)

The dairy industry has exploited cows and our environment to its limits, all in the name of cheap milk, resulting in the poor-quality dairy products now on the market. In the 1960s there were still some dual-purpose cows, good for beef and for milking.

66

The dairy industry has exploited cows and our environment to its limits

However, the rush to get big yields was underway. The dairy cow from Germany, the Holstein, was coming to the UK due to its massive milking capacity.

Despite the introduction of the Holstein, most cows at the time would have a calf every year and go on producing milk for 6 to 9 years. In stark contrast, now, most herds average no more than 3 to 4 lactations - in fact one study put it at 3.3. Cows are culled often in their first lactation year due to performance or health. This is truly disgraceful for such a wonderful animal.

Milk and health

Unpasteurised milk has many benefits. It is so much healthier for our gut and general health than pasteurised milk. The probiotic status of unheated raw milk supports good gut flora. One of the ways we can build our immunity and avoid allergies and asthma is by exposing ourselves to plenty of strong, vital, natural bacteria. This is particularly important for children, but is good for us at any age.

There was a time when the only milk we had was unpasteurised. Between the 1930s and the 1960s dairy hygiene was fairly basic by comparison with today, but this did not bring about much illness. In fact, it has often been said that this was a time of good diet, good health and strong immune systems.

There has been some concern surrounding TB in milk. However, many cows that test positive for TB are still healthy and so is the milk. Tens of thousands of animals with suspected TB are slaughtered each year and each one has an autopsy carried out. Evidence of illness is proved by TB lesions. If there are no lesions then the animal was simply a carrier

and may never have become ill at all. I know organic farmers who have had to have cows destroyed, only to find that test results later showed no lesions had been present.

Avoid homogenised milk, both organic and non-organic if you are able. Homogenisation blasts the milk and fat particles so they can no longer separate, making it easier for retailers to add shelf life and avoid so-called unsightly cream separation. This simply creates yet another challenge for our guts. The more we have messed with milk over recent times the more dairy intolerance in children has risen.

Calves need their mums

Farming can be tough, but we can do it with dignity and respect whether we are milking cows, sheep or goats. I have visited some excellent dairy farms where the calf has full access to its mum for several days, followed by a feed twice daily. Never being too far away from each other keeps both cow and calf happy.

There is so much marginal land that is not suitable for grain and pulse crops, but that can be used for careful animal husbandry. Good dairy farming for animals, environment and people may not be the cheapest way. However, compromising on this creates a system that is not very good for us, the cows or the environment.

Left: Patrick Holden at his organic farm. Right: The other end of the scale – an industrial dairy.

Tips

Tips for bringing sustainable dairy to your diet
Try and find a dairy producer, perhaps through your local organic shop. Find out who they are and how they farm. The more they depend on grass and not cereals the better the milk and cheese. Ask about how many months of the year they have daily access to grazing, It's good if, between April and November, cows are grazing at some point every day. It will depend on the type of soil on the farm just how many months they can stay out. Good practice will allow them out during the day for a few hours if conditions allow. It's much like us needing to go for a walk.

Milking and meat on a smallholding

At the Lothlorien community (see page 105), where from 1974 I ran our small holding livestock enterprise, I increased our dairy to three cows, plus calves, more pigs and plenty of chickens and ducks. I was also attempting to grow crops to feed them. We bought another couple of fields and after collecting and spreading muck from a nearby chicken farm, I had the field ploughed and sown with oats. The oats came up but along with them came a weed called redshank, which in the end dominated the crop so it was never going to be worth harvesting. I turned it into silage for winter feed for the cows.

I started to read books on organic farming, particularly Newman Turner, a pioneer of his time, alongside folk such as Sir Albert Howard who was considered to be the founding father of organic farming in the early 1940s. I also read John Seymour's *The Complete Book of Self-sufficiency* and Juliette de Bairacli Levy's *The Complete Herbal Handbook for Farm and Stable*. Ⓡ

There was so much to learn. With only these few books to guide me, I spent a lot of time observing and writing a diary, especially noting down the signs of fertility in the pastures. Depending on season and access, I also tried to make sure that the cows munched on a bit of tree foliage. Where they went in a field and what they left behind told me a lot about how I needed to farm in order to offer them the best diet.

My cows

Cows were of more interest to me. I loved them and they became a therapeutic part of my life. My cows (for they felt like mine) were Marigold the Guernsey, Roslyn an Ayrshire heifer with lovely horns and bull calf at foot, and Tansy a cross Ayrshire/Channel Island cow. They were my pride, my joy, and, at times, my life saver. Getting up early every day to milk them by hand. Feeling a bit sleepy and nuzzling into their flank to the sound of the warm milk hitting the sides of the stainless steel pail, leaving a milky smell in the air. There is nothing quite like being alone at 6 am nuzzled into the side of a cow. Now walking into a milking parlour takes me straight back. The smell of their breath and the noise of their hooves on concrete. They were treated so well, getting fabulous organic pasture every day as well as special rations for milking time. The cows would be content, eating a little wheat or barley, some bran flakes with a blob of molasses, and a splash of cider vinegar all to help keep them healthy. In the cold of the winter I would take some hot water and mix the bran and molasses together. It smelled very wholesome and I just knew my cows were smiling. When the cows came to have a calf, I was close and attentive giving them extra strokes. The calves were kept with their mums for two weeks, while I took the excess milk alongside them. You get to know fairly quickly what the calf needs to thrive and how much is left for you. After two weeks we would begin weening the calf slowly down to one feed a day. They were never far apart and this way everyone was happy.

These three cows provided all the milk for our community. It was a staple part of our food supply and we also used it to make cheese and butter. As Channel Island animals, two of them in particular gave high fat milk. We became spoilt for cream on our porridge, in apple crumbles and even on occasion in coffee.

Eating our own beef

One year at Lothlorien, the time came to kill a fatted calf. A two-and-a-half-year-old bull calf called Yarrow would be prime beef for us - a rare treat in those days. He was the offspring of Roslyn the wonderful wild looking Ayrshire dairy cow with fabulous horns she liked to shake at you to remind you she still had a wild nature at heart. The abattoir man arrived with his stun gun and we walked Yarrow up the field with his head in a bucket of feed. Bang. He knew nothing of it. Within 30 minutes we had a carcass of beef hoisted up using a block and tackle on an A-frame of poles. The carcass was skinned, halved and ready to hang to mature. I had brought this animal up since shortly after he was born and had loved him from his first wild days when he arrived with his Mum at the age of six weeks. I had cared for his welfare daily, but I was also fine with eating him. The celebrations that night eating fresh liver were wonderful and full of spirit and we gave thanks to the animal kingdom for feeding us.

Grazing for happy cows

The first field I sowed myself was full of meadow herbs such as plantain, chicory, clover, burnet, yarrow, as well as grasses such as cocksfoot, fescue, timothy and rye in parts. This was the best grazing and I sensed my cows smiling whenever I took them over to this field. It was also a field that could not be seen from the house and so offered me a little alone time. I would sit leaning into the side of Marigold as she lay chewing the cud of the herbal ley, feeling comforted by her smell and her breath.

The first August at Lothlorien in 1974, long before we had a herbal ley, brother Mark and I made meadow hay in a home field of permanent pasture using scythes and stooking it onto wooden tripods to dry. It was a wonderful experience and we were good at it. Sharpening them every 30 or 40 swings, learning to cut close to the sward, we earned plenty of blisters for our trouble, despite the already calloused hands. In later years and other fields a tractor mower belonging to our neighbour came to our rescue.

Veal

At Lothlorien, our animals were very healthy most of the time. However, there was a time when one of Marigold's calves got a bad foot and despite plenty

Beef bone stock

High in calcium, magnesium and phosphorous, homemade beef stock can boost the immune system and improve digestion. It also supports joints, hair, skin and nails due to its collagen content. Enjoy this as a drink on its own or as a base for soups and stews.

You will need a large (8-10 litre) stockpot for the quantity below.

Ingredients

2-3 kg of beef bones including marrow bone and/or tail
200 g onions cut in half, skin on
200 g carrot chunks, skin on
4 sticks celery
2 bay leaves
A handful of fresh herbs or a teaspoon of dried
1 tablespoon salt
1 teaspoon black peppercorns
1 tablespoon cider vinegar
4 cloves garlic

Roast the bones in the oven for about 30 minutes at 180 deg C. This gives the stock colour and improves the depth of flavour. Put the bones in your stock pot with the rest of the ingredients. Add water almost to the top of the pot and bring to the boil. Turn down the heat to a gentle simmer. Cook for at least two hours (three is good). Top up with water if you need to, but allow to reduce for the last hour so you get a rich stock that will form a jelly when cold.

of herbal remedies and poultices we were unable to heal it. We decided to call in the vet who suggested it would lose its foot and ought be put down. Off he went to the car to get his lethal injection. When he came back I asked him if the meat was alright to eat, to which he replied 'yes'. In that case, I said, I would like to keep it for meat. The vet left and I got a 6-inch nail and a lump hammer. I kissed the calf and talked to her before holding her gently between my legs and cleanly with one blow drove the nail into the spot that the vet had marked for me. It was done. I cried at the loss and at the relief. The calf was only 15 weeks old, but we had veal.

Food comes from the earth in the form of vegetables and animals. I am a human animal and enjoy all forms of food as my ancestors have before me. I wish to take responsibility for where my food comes from and not waste life. We feasted on the veal, giving thanks to the calf for its life and its nourishment of us.

If you wish to eat veal try to ensure it is pink veal only and from an organic farm where they leave the calf with its mother for much longer than the few hours that is normal in the industry. If you eat dairy it's perhaps worth thinking about the relationship between dairy and veal. We would do well to treat dairy like meat, seeking out only the very best from organic farms and try and give attention to its relationship with the land and the earth. The key for me is seeking close connection with your food. Know where the milk and meat come from, how they are produced. If you can, visit the farms and hear their story.

Why organic?

How the supermarkets compromised the organic movement

In the early 1990s, a Soil Association campaign to achieve a target of 20% of all food produced in the UK being organic by the year 2000 began. Although, with hindsight, this may seem crazily over-ambitious, it was a call to arms and led to some support for farmers wishing to convert to organic farming. Unfortunately, many of these farmers were probably doing it for the grants that were on offer, and when things got tough in the market again (partly due to the tactics of the supermarkets), these farmers reverted to chemical farming.

In 1986, a conference was held by British Organic Farmers (who were closely twinned with The Soil Association, even sharing a building in Colston Street in Bristol). The theme of the conference was 'Which Way Forward?': to build the independent market for organic produce or to use the supermarket scale to grow the market. As a small independent retailer, I naturally pushed for the former and said as much at the conference. I believed the market needed plenty of small independents and they needed the support of the institutions. Despite the many words of appreciation I received, particularly from small growers, sadly, the conference energy leaned towards the expansion of the market by using the supermarkets as the main route. We know that this growth was short lived and put many farmers out of business because of the way the supermarkets conducted their business.

Supermarkets played a huge part in the slowing of the organic market. We heard stories about up to 30% of a crop being rejected (think 'wonky carrots' or 'over-weight cabbages'). Lettuces with aphids were turned away commonly. Beef and lamb carcasses were penalised for fat content. All of this left a massive hole in farmers' accounts. It also led to disgraceful waste as these perfectly good products were carted away in skip loads to landfill.

Standards in organic farming

Although the organic market has grown a great deal since the 1980s, it still represents less than 3% of our total food consumed. A further issue is that some of the bigger organic farmers, while still maintaining organic certification, have joined the conventional market in scale and approach. I call this 'industrial organic farming'. Technically, yes, they comply with standards by not using chemicals and complying with animal welfare standards, but in terms of the benefits to wildlife habitat and soil health they maintain a lesser standard. To produce the very best food requires something almost intangible - love and connection with nature. This may seem a privileged position, but it's one we could all have the world over if the system was changed sufficiently. Following the Covid-19 pandemic, we know that we are capable of making huge change – and very quickly. The entire world's farming could be changed in a year or so if the political will was there. It is not, because it's too busy chasing the rules of capitalism.

Sacred soil

I now understand more fully what I believe to be important for us on Planet Earth in terms of food and farming. Soil has a spiritual and a sacred dimension. It's the crust of our earth that supports all life and we can feel that when we hold it in our hands. Food grown in soil that is cared for is deeply affected and energetically vibrant. It has a clean healthy and powerful path from soil to table to soul. Whether we eat this food consciously or not, it still impacts on life positively in a way that industrial and cosmetically perfect produce cannot. There is a life force and vitality that comes from food grown with love and a real care of nature.

As a grower myself I treat what I produce with honour and humility and it always tastes better. If you visit an allotment site, you will often find a happy place. Allotments are often quiet, as if all are busy in contemplation. They offer peace for our hearts because we are tending the place we come from and return to. We are simply outcrops of nature, borrowing every breath from the earth and returning it with thanks. To me the story of food is so very important. Even lesser quality food can be improved by touching it with love, care and a story on the way to our plate.

Carrots

There is something wonderful about carrots in September and October. They have had a full summer to grow and search deep into the soil for nutrients to transfer to the root. The best I have tasted came from a farm in West Wales belonging to Patrick Holden, a passionate carrot grower. In the days of the Organic Food Festival in Bristol, which used to happen at the start of September every year, Patrick would send us 500 bunches to sell. His soil had been organic since 1977. His carrots were sweet and with a real depth of flavour, grown with love and care for the soil.

Roasted carrots

Roasted carrots with love. Simple and sweet.

The carrot is the greatest symbol of good organic veg. When grown with love, carrots have the ability to bring the flavours and nutrients of the earth to life. I just adore this very simple way to cook them, which brings out all their sweetness and depth of flavour.

Take 1 kg of bunched carrots and wash them. When shopping, always choose dirty carrots over washed ones. Carrots covered in the soil they grew in have retained soul. Put them in a roasting tray and add olive oil and salt. I use a lot of salt (like 1 dessertspoon to the kilo of carrots) in this dish, but it's up to you and how you feel about salt. The salt draws out moisture and so intensifies the flavour. A lot of it is simply left in the pan.

Roast them at 180 deg C. Test to see how they are after 15 minutes although you may find they need closer to 30 minutes, depending on carrot type, size and even the time of year.

I love these next to a really creamy potato mash, but they make a wonderful warm salad as well if you add a drizzle of lemon juice.

Sicilian adventure

Part of our Sicily tour

A quest for blood orange juice

In 2016, after our supplier of delicious blood orange juice suddenly disappeared from the market without trace, I was on a hunt for a good organic juice that fitted with our values. Despite there being plenty of fantastic organic orange growers in Europe, this was proving difficult.

I started reading about blood oranges and their extra nutritional benefits, especially those grown around Mount Etna. After a bit of research, I found a group of organic and biodynamic farmers in Sicily who had a juicing plant. This sounded like a trip. It seemed quite impossible to go and see orange growers in Sicily without spending time exploring the island, its foods, its culture and meeting a few of its people. Hurray for hard work!

Easter in Sicily

Easter 2017 saw my wife, Gerry, and I off on a two-week itinerary with food and sea at its heart. This turned out to be a fabulously rich experience, steeped in old culture, forgotten landscapes and the most delightful and generous people one could imagine. And that was before the food or juice experience!

For the Easter weekend we headed west for the coast. On Good Friday, Gerry led the way to some culture in Trapani by way of an extraordinary spectacle – the Misteri Parades – a day-long procession featuring 20 floats of life-size wood and canvas sculptures portraying stations of the cross. Along with each float were musicians playing wind and brass, all repetitive, slow marches, each band competitively representing a region and delivering every step with a mix of pride and tradition.

The sea offered fabulous swimming, with crystal blue water and rocky picnic places. The hills, filled with native flowers, cattle and sheep made for long walks. We feasted our senses on the colours, smells and breathtaking views.

A simple but massive food highlight for me was the whole lemons picked from the tree and eaten before breakfast. A zingy wake up that I got addicted to, leaving me feeling a little righteous and very awake.

We crossed the island over to the east to the hills close to Taormina where we had some divine food moments.

My favourite bit was the globe artichokes. Unlike in the UK, where they are expensive, there is a special

89

Nuts and spices in
a Sicilian market

magic about the abundance of these local fresh Sicilian ones. From field to market to me to pot, out of the pot, olive oil, pepper and of course squeezed lemon. Job done.

Our accommodation being somewhat lacking in fresh water, I went many times to get water which was safe to use. Below us was a hillside of old terraces for growing food on with intricate waterways, mostly all ruined and disused, but still flowing in at the top and being channelled to various small orange groves. This was water from the volcanic hills behind us looking up towards Mount Etna.

Agrinova citrus growers

Our next stop was to visit our citrus growers cooperative Agrinova in their orange groves near Mount Etna. We chose these growers because of the qualities of the blood oranges grown in the black volcanic soils of the area. These soils are rich in minerals and trace elements including anthocyanins, which help the oranges turn red. The unique climate of the area, particularly the extreme temperature difference between day (eg 20 deg C) and night (-2 deg C), help to sweeten the orange. With a cold winter you get the very best blood oranges in the world.

By including precious molecules like anthocyanins in our daily diet, which act as powerful antioxidants, we maintain our body's defences, we protect our cells against ageing and we guard against the loss of our vitality. Nothing can chase away the winter blues better than a dose of Sicily's arance rosse, the 'red oranges' commonly known as blood oranges. Sicily produces three varieties of arance rosse that are protected under the PGI (Protected Geographical Indication) certification attributed to heirloom products from a specific area. We now stock this juice in all our stores when in season.

When we arrived at the farm there were half a dozen workers climbing short ladders picking oranges, filling crates full and stacking them ready for the short trip into the juicing house a mere 100 metres away. This was a state-of-the-art factory on the farm for both a frozen juice product and essential orange oils. Standing in the grove watching them pick, I ate a couple of oranges off the tree. It was about 25 degrees in the sun and as I bit into the skin of the orange, the scent of the oils exploded in my face. Followed by the devouring of those warm juicy orange segments, this was a moment I will feast on in my mind for ever more.

We feasted our senses on the colours, smells and breathtaking views

Blood orange salad with chicory

The blood orange season is December to May and I find they taste best from February to April. It's the Tarcocco orange that has a beautiful deep colour, but you can also use Moro, or Sanguinello. The prime season for buying chicory is January to March, which makes this the perfect time for this dish.

It's a very simple salad, but you need to cut the orange the right way.

Using a sharp knife on a wooden board cut the top off an orange and then cut round top to nearly bottom and carry on doing this all the way round the fruit until you have a sort of flower of orange peel still attached at the bottom, then cut the bottom off. Do all this over a a large bowl to catch the juices.

Now hold the orange cradled in one hand and cut between the membranes of each segment towards the centre and leave the segment in place for now. Carry on doing this all the way around so you get lovely segments with zero pith. Once all segments have been prised away from the main fruit, you can squeeze the remaining juice into the bowl. Use as many oranges as the number of people you are feeding. Take one average chicory head to each orange and cut across the head in slices. When you get close to the bottom, if you like you could turn the head and slice it very thinly.

Toss in some walnuts and add walnut oil or olive oil if you prefer, and finally a small amount of good fruit vinegar. A grind of pepper is a nice addition.

You will have a wonderfully seasonal and delicious salad!

The bounty and beauty of Sicily

The rest of our trip through Sicily included a romantic time in Syracuse down on the south east coast – such a beautiful town with a market to feast your senses. It was impossible not to buy too much. We ate lunch in a fabulous deli restaurant in the market, ridiculously bustling and busy, crammed with cheese, meats, wines and salads all making our hearts sing and our stomachs crave. All, fast, simple and such a celebration of what this earth's crust offers us.

Unable to resist heading back to the market the following day, we came across a stall selling freshly made arancini. These were the real deal, with fresh herbs in the rice mix and moist spinach and pine nuts in the centre, seasoned with nutmeg and pepper.

Syracuse, Sicily

Arancini

Arancini are essentially a street food, like an alternative to a sandwich, although certainly best served warm. They are delicious at home too! There are a couple of ways to make arancini, one using boiled rice. However, this version starts with a risotto, which I think offers more depth of flavour.

Ingredients

For the rice balls
1 onion chopped finely
30 to 40 g grated parmesan
1 lemon using both zest and juice
olive oil
250 g risotto rice
1 small pinch of saffron
About 80 ml dry white wine
1 litre hot vegetable stock, preferably fresh and organic, or, as arancini are a robust tasty street food, I think using bouillon is fine.
Oil for frying (I use Clearspring sunflower frying oil rather than cold pressed, which I find too strong)

For the filling
It's up to you. You could make a stiff bolognaise out of minced pork, but my favourite is with wild mushrooms.

150 g wild or ordinary mushrooms
2 cloves garlic
1 teaspoon tomato puree
150g any good, local, flavoursome cheese.
Salt and pepper

For coating
80 g plain flour
1 or 2 free-range eggs whisked up with a fork
150 g fine dried breadcrumbs

Method

Drizzle some olive oil into a large pan over a low heat, add the onions and cook for 15 minutes or until soft but not coloured.

Turn the heat up to medium, add the rice and stir for a few minutes until all the rice grains are coated, then add the saffron and stir well.

Pour in the wine and let it bubble away for a couple of minutes, stirring regularly. Start adding the stock bit by bit, stirring it through the rice and allowing each amount to become absorbed before adding the next bit. Continue until the rice is cooked through – about 15 to 20 minutes.

Add the grated Parmesan and a squeeze of lemon juice, then leave to cool while you make the filling.

Chop the mushroom and garlic very finely and sauté lightly in olive oil with a little salt. Cook until juices run a little, then add tomato puree, mix well, take off the heat and add grated cheese.

To form the arancini, scoop a portion of the cooled risotto into your hand. Spoon 1 dessertspoon of the filling mixture into the centre and wrap the risotto around it to seal completely. Repeat with the remaining risotto and filling.

To coat, place the flour, beaten eggs and breadcrumbs into separate shallow bowls. Dip each arancini ball into the flour, then the egg, and finally the crumbs, ensuring the rice is completely coated. Set aside.

Pour enough vegetable oil into a deep, heavy-bottomed saucepan that will just cover the arancini and place over a high heat. To test that the oil is hot enough, drop in a few breadcrumbs – if they sizzle and float, it is ready.

Carefully lower in the arancini with a slotted spoon and deep-fry for about 8 minutes, or until golden and crispy. Using a spoon with holes transfer to a double layer of kitchen paper to drain.

A fantastic summer picnic food.

The joys of growing your own

After a very cold spring the garden is coming on. Yet, I have lost a bit of confidence in the so-called seasons. I think we are being pushed by climate chaos to be more reactive these days, rather than being able to plan by the calendar.

Time outside. Open the gate, cultivate, rake and sow. Onions up, broad beans flowering, rhubarb going bonkers, potatoes showing first green, last of the baby leeks ready to bolt, and the delight of the first asparagus on a plate last night.

In the greenhouse, still too much chard, old parsley going into flower mode, strawberries in full flower and a fine looking pea crop under way. I love the early carrots I will pick as bunches in late May and the beetroot for salads. Tomatoes are doing fine but zero germination of aubergines this year.

So many seedlings almost ready to go out. Brassicas, beans, celeriac, squash, courgette, sweetcorn and more.

It is a wonderful thing to have your own garden or allotment. Your own produce always tastes so much better than anything else you will ever eat. My vegetable patch and greenhouse are a place for me to get lost in and for me to be still with what is right now. The birds around me know who I am and what I am doing.

The soil knows me and is strong in its simple work and with its infinite wisdom.

Breathe and be nourished. Be grateful and be attentive.

The greatest action we can all take to mend our food system is to grow our own food, be that in a window box, a garden, an allotment or by joining a shared growing project.

Tips

Growing your own vegetables

A greenhouse or small polytunnel can lengthen the season if you are lucky enough to have the space for one. If you cover the soil to keep it warm you can start as early as late January, putting in lettuce, turnips, beetroot, or carrots.

Sow these early crops with big spaces between them to allow for planting your tomatoes later on in May.

At the other end of the season when the tomatoes are ready to harvest, sow green manure or perhaps carrots, salads and even potatoes for a late crop for Christmas. Keep feeding with good garden compost.

In winter on the allotment, keep your soil covered with plants as much as possible. You can also use old compost sacks and the like as ground cover to keep weeds down. I find this makes it easier to use no-dig methods outside. ®

Fiona Provan
The Calf at Foot Dairy

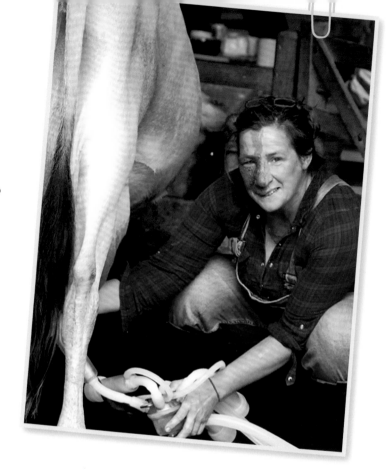

What can you do to support better and more responsible food production? Buy produce from the smaller producer who sells whole real food direct to the end consumer, cutting out any middlemen. This way you know every penny in every pound goes straight to the farmer. Unfortunately, the better food producers are few and far between right now. A truly genuine small or micro producer probably will not have the funds to advertise through mainstream media.

However, now we have social media it's easy to find these small producers because platforms such as Facebook are free and easy for us to promote our wares. Small-scale food production is making a comeback from backyard growers, allotments with the occasional glut to share with their neighbours, smallholders with the odd pig, a house cow and a handful of hens, to micro-dairies such as ours with a handful of house cows, selling our produce to make a living.

My first mission was to prove it's possible to farm dairy cows without cruelty by allowing them to keep their calves, giving them a stress-free living environment without fear or pain. Secondly, I wanted to farm regeneratively, looking after the soil and the biosphere for future generations. Thirdly, I wished to make sure my produce is as nutritionally dense as possible by allowing the cows a natural diet – in other words, grass. And finally, my ambition was to pass on my methods, encouraging others to produce milk in the same way. I pioneered the Calf at Foot dairying methods (for more on this see our website).

There is a quiet agrarian revolution of responsible regenerative farming taking place. For the good of our health and our planet, this movement has to be supported and the only way to support it is through the pound in your pocket. Yes, proper good food may seem expensive, but if we re-prioritise and make food our first go-to above all else, we can support the good farmers and before long there will be more popping up in every community, rural and urban, which will eventually cut down on delivery costs. Never forget, there is no such thing as cheap food – something's got to give whether it's your health or the planet's.

Resources
Better farm and grow

Organisations for better farming and growing

Community Supported Agriculture (CSA)
communitysupportedagriculture.org.uk

Incredible Edible Todmorden project
incredible-edible-todmorden.co.uk

Soil Association
soilassociation.org

Garden Organic
gardenorganic.org.uk

Sustainable Food Trust
sustainablefoodtrust.org

Books

de Bairacli Levy, Juliette (1991) *The Complete Herbal Handbook for Farm and Stable*, Faber and Faber

Diacono, Mark (2013) *Chicken & Eggs: River Cottage Handbook No.11*, Bloomsbury.

Dowding, Charles (2010) *Organic Gardening: The natural no-dig way, 2nd Edn*, Green Books

Hill, Lawrence (1973) *Grow Your Own Fruit and Vegetables*, Faber and Faber

Hill, Lawrence (1977) *Organic Gardening*, Penguin

Qure, Sandy (2015) *Organic Square Foot Gardening for Beginners*, CreateSpace

Seymour, John (1978) *The Complete Book of Self-sufficiency*, Corgi

Tree, Isabella, (2019) *Wilding: The return of nature to a British farm*, Picador.

Turner, Newman (2009) *Fertility Farming*, Acres USA

Turner, Newman (2009) *Fertility Pastures*, Acres USA

Articles, blogs, web

BBC (2016) 'EU referendum: Did 1975 predictions come true?', bbc.co.uk/news/uk-politics-36367246. (accessed 12 June 2020)

EPA 'DDT - A Brief History and Status', epa.gov/ingredients-used-pesticide-products/ddt-brief-history-and-status (accessed 4 May 2020)

Hansard (1960) 'Farm workers (lifting of weights)', HC Deb 10 February 1960 vol 617 cc599-616

Soil Association, Organic Poultry – Keeping Chickens and Other Poultry Organically, soilassociation.org/organic-living/why-organic/better-for-animals/poultry-chickens (accessed 12 June 2020)

The Guardian (accessed 27 April 2020) 'Raw milk: a superfood or super risky?' - theguardian.com/lifeandstyle/2017/may/30/raw-milk-health-superfood-safety-goop

The Poultry Pages, chickens.allotment-garden.org/organic-poultry (accessed 12 June 2020)

Uberoi, Elise (2019) 'Bovine TB Statistics: Great Britain', House of Commons Briefing Paper Number 6081, 22 July, https://researchbriefings.files.parliament.uk/documents/SN06081/SN06081.pdf (accessed 10 June 2020)

Better community

Connecting with each other
for the wellbeing of our
culture and society

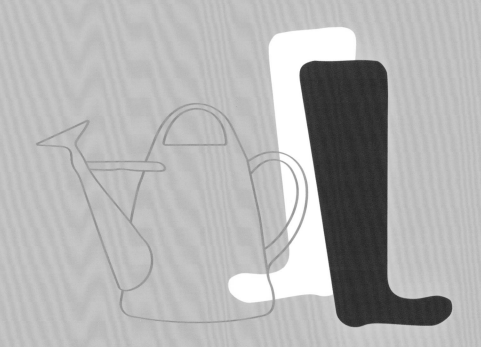

Community is the place we grow hearts and minds, where we foster generosity, where we sometimes compromise for the greater good, and where we feel a sense of belonging. Being a part of a good community in any form offers security and at its best becomes our hearth and home.

It seems to me that there is a big difference between the way we experienced community 50/60 years ago and the way we do today. Our values as a society with regards to consumerism have shifted significantly, our family habits have transformed out of recognition, our pace of life is faster and stresses are more complex. Growing up in the 1960s the communities around me had a strong sense of self-confidence and family, school and village were all highly valued. However, those same communities now seem anxious, insecure, divided. Families themselves even lack time to share meals and have slow downtime together.

Now that we are moving into a new era for humanity, we are questioning the wisdom of our choices around oil, plastic, social media, supermarkets, fast food and fast fashion and chemical farming, to name just a few. We can learn from our past about what was more nourishing for humanity and what helped us feel safe within our communities. It's time to rebuild communities in order to mend our broken culture with a renewed spirit of hope.

Phil talked to... Rosemary Haughton and Nancy Schwoyer

Nancy and Rosemary are among seven people who founded a community called Wellspring House in Gloucester, Massachusetts in 1981, committed to work for justice through the practice of hospitality.

Phil: What is important to you about community?

Rosemary and Nancy: It is a biological fact that humans are wired for connection. Each one of us is dependent on the other, physically, emotionally, intellectually and spiritually. We are made to live interdependently not only with each other but with all living things.

The organisation we, and others, founded in Massachusetts and lived with for 35 years expressed its identity in the mission statement: 'Wellspring is a community of faith' (that is, not a separate religious tradition, but a conviction) 'aware that each life touches every other life. Our work is guided by the vision of a just society in which we must care for the earth and her people in a spirit of hospitality...'. Hospitality is of central importance to us and we believe is essential to the nature of community because it requires risk, trust and honesty. In practice, this hospitality led us to offer shelter to homeless families and to develop a variety of community educational programmes. We also developed affordable housing and advocated 'Housing for All' at the local, state and national levels. We grew vegetables and food, which was prepared and shared daily as well as during every celebration.

Community matters to us because we are learning to be human. What is important to us in living community are the four Cs: Commitment to a communitarian model of organisation, Convening regularly to reflect on our work and plan for the future, Connecting with others as partners and resources and Celebrating our unity and humanity.

Phil: What are your suggestions for how people can do/act/work to make change in the world?

Rosemary and Nancy: Our experience leads us to believe that the making of real change has to be driven by grief and outrage at what is wrong combined with compassion in making the change. The passion for a remedy for oppression and callousness in society becomes effective through the right kind of organising. When the coronavirus of 2020 began to spread fear and grief all over the world some people reacted by buffering themselves. Others organised themselves to ensure the most vulnerable got essential food. Yet, just as important as the food was the friendship, the laughter and the ingenuity. During this time neighbourhoods recognised themselves as communities reclaiming their roles as citizens and called the governments to account for their decisions and actions.

Crisis is the gateway to opportunity, and even though the gate is heavy, we must push it open. At the time we are talking, in May 2020, all over the world ordinary people are gathering to reflect on this question. We are all thinking about what we have learned from the experience of this crisis and imagining the new reality we want to create together. In planning for change we believe that it is essential to be in touch with our past, our history, and our memories. What was significant in making our present and the world in which we live today? What do we want to discard? What do we want to take into the future? We can imagine a different future, and what we can imagine we can make.

Phil: What do our leaders and governors need to do to help make change?

Rosemary and Nancy: What our leaders and governments need to do is to listen to the people, and to cooperate and support citizen assemblies or other local, regional and national gatherings where people meet to imagine a future that is communitarian and equitable, just and compassionate. People in positions of authority, whether by election or opportunity, need to learn the humility to join with those they lead to shape a better future. They must shift from exercising power 'over' to power 'with'. This will require humility and a lot of unlearning. In the years ahead the future of the earth depends on the ability of her leaders – political, financial and cultural – to learn the skills of exercising 'power with'.

Mum's bread

Ingredients

Flour, salt, yeast, water and hands

Method

Put wholewheat flour in a big bowl, add salt. Mix yeast with warm water and add to a well in the flour. When it bubbles add water to make a dough that doesn't stick to your hands. Knead until smooth and elastic. Clean the bowl and coat with olive oil. Put dough back in the bowl, cover with a damp cloth and leave to rise. Grease bread tins. When dough is risen, knock back and knead a little more, re-cover and let it rise. (It's good to do this twice.) Shape dough into loaves and put in tins. Let prove 30–60 minutes under a cloth until risen to just proud of the edge of the tins. Bake at 200 deg C (or less in a fan oven) for 35–40 minutes or until loaves sound hollow when tapped.

Cool on racks.

Community starts with family

Eating together as a family

In the 1960s our family weekday suppers were good old English staples that Mum was very good at. Shepherd's pie (with baked beans to pad it out), suet dumplings in gravy, macaroni cheese or potato cheese, both using blocks of cheddar from the cash and carry, to which a monthly trip to stock up on staples helped make ends meet. On these occasions the pantry, a converted shower room with metal wracking, would suddenly appear full of goodies. Mum would also stock the fridge with butter, which my brother Luke liked to eat like a bar of chocolate. Mum's own food fetish was for Philadelphia soft cheese. Meat and dumplings, and of course bubble and squeak with leftovers from the Sunday roast were regularly dished up. If we were lucky there might be stewed apple and custard for pudding. Also bread and butter pudding was a staple, made from left over brown bread, sultanas, brown sugar and milk with an egg in it. Can't beat it, hot or cold.

All these meals were eaten at our family table, or rather two family tables, because age and school divided us, so often weekdays there was sister Lizzy, Luke and myself for supper. Mum would wait for Dad to get home later in the evening.

Our evenings were a set routine. Home from school to go out to play, or watch a bit of children's telly if we were lucky, then chores such as hoovering, ironing, cleaning the bathroom and so on before supper. Then, after washup, we would do our handy work like readicut rugs, basketwork or tapestry. We did all this while listening to Mum reading books to us such as a Dickens or Tolkien.

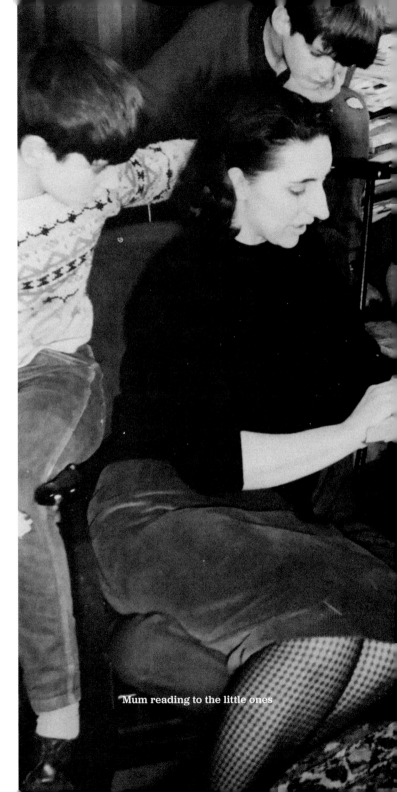

Mum reading to the little ones

Shepherd's pie

This dish started life as a Sunday roast leftover dish. The joint would have been cut into small chunks and minced in a hand mincer. (You might still find one of these in a junk shop.) The meat would have been lamb or mutton (being the meat appropriate for a shepherd), but over the years it has become confused with cottage pie which is made with beef. So think of this dish as a delicious dish made from any fresh minced meat, or as a versatile way of using up leftovers. The key to this recipe is to use less meat. My recipe is not really traditional and never the same twice.

Feeds 4 to 6

400 g minced lamb or beef or leftover roast meat (put through a mincer or carefully chop and re-chop to get a course mince). If you are using fresh raw mince just cook it for longer after adding to the onions.

1 large onion chopped
2 cloves garlic chopped
200 g carrots diced small
1 tin baked beans
1 teaspoon dried mixed herbs
A bay leaf
1 dessertspoon paprika
1 teaspoon salt and ½ teaspoon black pepper

Method

Sauté the onions and garlic with the herbs until they soften, around 4 to 6 minutes. Turn the heat up, add the mince and allow to heat through. Add carrots, bay leaf, paprika, beans and salt and pepper.

Add a cupful of water (or stock of some kind to lift the flavour even more), and allow to simmer gently for about 15 minutes or until the mix is the right consistency to take a crust of mashed potato.

For the mash, boil 1 kg potatoes until soft. Preheat your oven to 200 deg C while the potatoes are boiling. Drain them and add some butter and milk plus lots more black pepper if you like it and mash really well.

Place the meat mixture into an ovenproof dish of about 200 x 300 cm. Spread your potato over the top smoothly, then use a fork to make little ridges. You could brush a bit of oil lightly over the top to help form a crust.

Cook for about 30 minutes. To ensure a nice crisp top, place the pie under a hot grill for another 5 minutes or so until the crust has the colour and crispness you want.

I love lots of greens with this dish.

Village communities in the 1960s

Made to last

In the village of Gilling, where I lived as a small boy, there was a cobbler, Mr Suggit, who mended everyone's shoes and boots. At this time it was normal to have only a few pairs of shoes that would last a long time and be re-soled many, many times while being handed down through the family as we grew. Shoes were made with leather soles and plenty of little replaceable nails and they lasted years and years. Perhaps ours was the last generation where quality and longevity were part of manufacturing pride, before it became the norm to expect cheaper items designed to have short life spans so we needed to come back sooner to buy again. This change in our culture has played a huge role in pollution, carbon emissions and waste issues. When I was a child, mending and darning were commonplace, as were leather patches on jumper elbows – now only seen as a design feature.

Mr Suggit mended all our shoes and, in the same workshop, he also cut hair. They were pretty crude haircuts, pudding bowl style, like the Beatles!

The sad demise of the railways

The village had a railway station whose days were numbered thanks to the Beeching railway cuts. This station was used for many goods to be transported to other parts of the country – we used to send parcels from it ourselves. Small, slow, countryside trains stopped at many villages between towns. I am sure that the costs of labour to keep all these stations alive would have seemed mad economics as cars started to dominate and motorways began to be built, but cars introduced sweeping changes in employment patterns, social interactions, infrastructure and the distribution of goods. It's sad now to see that infrastructure gone for ever at a time when we are seriously questioning the wisdom of clogging up our roads and cities with combustion engines. Until the mid 1900s we mostly used buses and trains, bikes, and feet. Use of cars today has a huge impact on society and more urgently climate chaos. During the Covid-19 lockdown in 2020 we have seen and felt the benefit to our health and wellbeing of fewer cars on the roads. We have proved that we can change to something better very quickly if we really want to.

Lothlorien – the building of a community

New beginnings

In 1972, after a family meeting at our home in Yorkshire it was decided to look for a new venture and an escape from the somewhat dysfunctional life of Ampleforth College. The plan was to drop out of the rat race, to build a new home and create a self-sufficient, back-to-the-land life for any family and friends looking to join us. For me, this new home and extraordinary project would be a game changer in so many ways. Lothlorien would shape my working life and mission more than any other chapter in my life.

We found 9 acres of woodland and fields in Galloway, a Scottish county consisting of small, rolling, green hills called drumlins and woods crisscrossed by stone dykes built to serve as farm field boundaries for keeping stock in. I hold deep gratitude to our country farmers for the walls they built - they represent a true statement of permanence and purpose.

Above these drumlins the landscape climbed up to moorland hills at about 600 feet above sea level. Our closest village was Corsock in the heart of drumlin country. The more substantial hill village of Moniave lay about 8 miles to the north at the foot of higher, more craggy hills. All around the drumlins were peaty bogs and marsh grass. The farmed drumlins were used for grass and arable. The crops were barley, oats, sheep turnips and kale for cattle. In those days, kale wasn't seen as food for humans, although it has become a green that we all rave about now. The fields turned up endless stones every time they were ploughed and these were used to build the stone wall field boundaries. I spent days helping to clear fields of these stones before they could be drilled with seed.

Benet working on the log house

A typical farm size in the 1970s would have been 200 acres and it would have supported mainly sheep and cattle. The local cattle were a real mix, but Belted Galloway were the hardy locals in that area. They were able to stay out all winter alongside the Scottish Blackface sheep.

Lothlorien was bought with land and planning permission, including logs to build a home, from a couple of Canadians who had planned to build and make a new life but had to return to Canada. The site consisted of a muddy track up which there was a 30-foot caravan for my brother Nic and his wife Pauline, a cluster of strong wooden sheds and a woodcutter's caravan tucked into the woods of mostly silver birch and oak.

A motley crew, no running water, no electricity...

Lothlorien, 1976

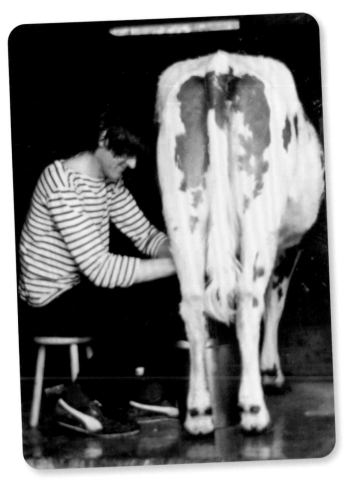

Setting up home and finding happiness with the animals

So here we were. A motley crew, no running water, no electricity, just two caravans and a few sheds on the edge of a small wood. And a huge pile of fresh cut trees to build a house. We had no idea about how to farm and produce food, but we would end up just getting on with it anyway.

We set about making camp-style life as comfortable as possible. We worked hard, building a garden from a very rocky corner of the land and over the next few months, with some advice from Willie Gordon, the neighbouring farmer who had sold the field originally, we bought pigs and put them in a shed and chickens that were good at getting up into the trees instead of their coop at night and that would prove marginal at providing us with eggs. And a cow called Marigold. Marigold was a Guernsey who was placid and provided us with plenty of milk. Of course, Willie may have been on the make and we probably paid well over the odds for everything, although at the time we felt he was doing us a great favour. Actually, he was a good teacher in many ways for us green, middle-class, back-to-the-landers.

I knew as soon as I arrived that this move was truly wonderful. I knew in my heart I could be a farmer and felt a huge sense of purpose. I was as happy as a pig in shit!

Pigs don't really like being in shit at all. Given the right conditions and amount of space, they like to be meticulously clean, particularly with regard to their toilet habits, choosing a particular corner to shit and pee, always ensuring it is well away from their bed area.

In April of 1974 I joined some of the family who had already moved to Lothlorien. I turned 17 on the 22nd of that month. On the morning of my birthday, it was unusually warm and sunny. I found a tin bath and put it out in a clearing in the wood in front of where the house was going to be built and began heating water on the arctic stove in the shed 50 yards away. The stove was a bit less than a metre high and barrel shaped with top loading for the wood. After a couple of trips with hot water I took my bath. Washing myself out in open nature, feeling the light breeze on my body, filled my heart with gladness on that warm sunny day. My life was going to be good.

It was my job to feed our two pigs, Sid and Eike, named after the two crazed woodcutters down in the village. Sid and Eike were housed in a new garden shed in a corner paddock enclosed by the stone dykes. Our pigs smelt good and piggy, were friendly, with inquisitive noses. They made delightful grunts of appreciation when you scratched them behind the ears. I also milked Marigold and revelled in the sense of purpose this gave me. Cow eats grass, comes to milking shed early morning and early evening, provides creamy delicious milk that we enjoy every day. What could be better?

Getting down to basics

In August of 1974 the mobile home some of the family had lived in in Yorkshire was transported to its new site at Lothlorien. It was placed close to our biggest shed and we made a porch between them from corrugated plastic sheets and pine poles. We even found an old Rayburn, which we installed in the porch area to help with cooking and hot water for washing. The loo was a sort of wigwam with a pit and some boards, with earth to throw in after you'd done your business.

All water came from a well on the other side of the woods. To start with we used buckets on ropes to retrieve water. Then we bought a hand pump and spent hours a day pumping water into big cans that we carried back across the wood. We added a hose that went all the way across the wood and into a water butt above the caravan. This was a day of celebration. We now had running water coming out of a tap inside the caravan. Pumping was a chore undertaken by everyone on a rota and, for me, usually done while reading. It was quiet and peaceful, but when winter came that first year the pipes froze and we had to go back to carrying buckets across the woods and we lost our 'tap'. So we dug a wiggly trench with pick and shovel right across the wood to bury the hosepipe. After weeks of this we had a better system that gave us a supply of cold water to the main caravan year round. It was still pretty primitive. The day came when the pump was too much like hard work so we bought a small diesel pump. What had taken an hour to pump was now done in less than five minutes.

A few years on and our 10-bedroom house had a generator to give us electricity. We could read by electric light. We could iron our clothes. We were able to use power tools. It may have just been for about three hours each evening, but it was all we needed and life was good.

Building the house

Building a large house out of local logs was mad, hard work and also a lot of fun. Green logs freshly cut from the local forests arrived shortly after we did but they needed stacking and curing for at least a year before stripping of all their bark. Thousands of pegs had to be made using a draw knife and sitting on a draw horse whittling away for hours.

We had block and tackles everywhere as the house went up and up. There were plenty of people involved in the building, and everybody needed good food to keep them going. Mark headed up the garden, carving out a corner of productive vegetable growing from what seemed more like a quarry.

I concentrated on the milk, meat and eggs, supplying the protein for our diets.

Creating a community

The huge undertaking of the Lothlorien project attracted many people. For most involved it was an exciting new way to live on the land and build and work together. Part of our purpose was always to offer hospitality to any visitors, which, alongside a strong work ethic, was written into our family DNA. My brothers Benet and Mark took the lead as master builder and head gardener respectively, Mum was the vision guide, and Dad, who seemed to be happy for the first time in many years, gave his life to the kitchen, the building and the accounts. I was, of course, the farmer.

The community was home to between 12 and 40 people, depending on the time of year. There was a sort of management team who met to talk about community business. There soon came a time when there was no money. Teams of us needed to go out to work in the woods for the Forestry Commission to earn the cash to keep feeding everyone and to keep building the huge log house. This meant planting conifer trees up steep bleak hillsides often in terrible weather. Thousands of trees had to be planted each day in order to make our quota and get paid a reasonable amount. It was soul-destroying work but we needed the dosh.

Cutting down trees that others had planted some 20 to 40 years before was somehow more engrossing, even if rather brutal, and we did plenty of this too. First and second thinnings that we then dragged out of the woods with our horse Captain, a lovely Welsh cob. A horse was commonly used for this purpose in these conifer forests at the time. We also had a tractor and winch, which I disliked using. Working with Captain was a privilege, although very hard work as you had to concentrate hard. Captain thought the best way to get these logs out of the woods was to charge at it, perhaps assuming that momentum would make lighter work of it. However, we wanted him to walk so we could control the path and avoid damage to

him down. I rode him hard from the paddock up the hill for a mile to where we were working, then took him straight into pulling logs – each around 30 to 40 feet long. On his first load he took off, just as I was catching on the last of the logs. As he charged off the logs swung round and hit my leg hard enough to knock me over and I hurt my back falling backwards down the hill. I learnt a salutary lesson that day about safety and from then on tied Captain to the nearest tree until I was ready for us to walk on.

Food for our sustenance and our celebrations

Our 'piece', or food box was a hugely important part of the day in the woods. After leaving home very early and often driving for up to an hour to the site, we were ready for our first bite by about 9.30 am. A thermos of tea and a cheese and onion sandwich were normally the order of the day. The sandwich was made from our best homemade wholemeal bread with Scottish mature block cheddar, sliced onions and black pepper. To this day I love a good moist wholemeal cheese and onion sandwich. If we were lucky we had ginger cake or the like for a bit of sweet stuff. These packed lunches were often kindly made for us the night before, so we knew we were well supported in our quest to keep the wheels going for the community.

Sunday was a day of rest, relatively speaking, although the cows still had to be milked and general chores done. Dad continued the family tradition of making white bread rolls for breakfast so he was always up very early to prove and bake them. Eaten hot from the oven, these made a great breakfast with our own churned butter and Dad's homemade

standing trees. Penalties for debarking standing trees while dragging logs out were hefty and could easily eat into your pay cheque. Captain had a huge metal collar and my job, after attaching the logs to chains and to his harness gear, was to hold his head leathers and walk him out, often up and down and across steep hills.

One spring morning I went to get Captain from his field. He was very frisky on the spring grass. It took ages to catch him and then I knew I needed to calm

66
Working with Captain,
a lovely Welsh cob,
was a privilege

marmalade. Made from fresh Seville oranges, it was thick cut chunky style and with less sugar than standard recipes.

Along with the difficult times at Lothlorien, there were also times for celebration and this we did with energy and delight. It was a huge joy to eat together – often as many as 40 of us. In the summer we would eat outside under tarpaulins, with all the food prepared in the tiny caravan kitchen with its outdoor porch. At that time of year there would be many visitors helping to build the house. Outdoor fires were common, with people sitting round playing music, drinking and smoking rollups and the odd joint of home-grown grass.

There were times we had so little money that meals would consist of porridge and toast for breakfast, pearl barley soup for lunch and rice and roasted swede for supper. In the winter before the house was complete, we ate in a shed next to the caravan. There were many feasts – Christmas dinner, an Easter feast, birthdays and one notable christening delivered by Father Anthony, a great old family friend who ran a Sirenian shelter in Edinburgh among other Christian causes. Ben and Kaaren had recently had their son, Theo, and in the middle of the service Ben grabbed hold of me while Father Anthony asked me to repeat his words. I was now a godfather.

I will always look back at Lothlorien as a formative time of my life in food, farming and community. Above all I learned the value of working together in a living community with a strong sense of purpose.

Dad's marmalade

Dad loved marmalade and was the master marmalade maker in a house of up to 30 people. Marmalade takes quite a while to make, but you can stop and start the process if you need to.

Some tips first:

The oranges: Seville (organic of course) – have a strong sour and bitter flavour that can bear the addition of lots of sugar without becoming sickly sweet.

The sugar: most recipes call for twice as much sugar per weight of oranges, but 1½ times the weight of sugar to oranges works for me.

The lemons: 2 or 3 for every kilo of oranges helps with setting when using less sugar.

The pan: the bigger the better, preferably nice and wide.

Some recipes don't pre-cook the oranges, but my Dad's method of doing so makes it easier to scoop out the flesh and pith and slice the skins, without juice going everywhere.

Ingredients

2 kg organic Seville oranges
4 to 5 organic lemons
3 kg organic granulated sugar

This will make a total weight of 5 kg-ish. That's about 12 large jam jars. Halve the recipe if this is too much.

Method

Put all the oranges and lemons in the pan with about 4 pints of water or enough to cover them. Don't worry about them bobbing above the water line. Bring to the boil. Put a lid on the pan and boil until the orange skins are softened (around 30 to 40 minutes). This step can be done the night before.

Line a large mixing bowl with a muslin cloth, letting the edges hang down the outside of the bowl.

When the fruits are cool enough to handle, lift them out, leaving the liquid in the pan. Halve all the fruit crossways. Pick out the pips and drop them into the muslin-lined bowl, then scoop all the flesh and pith into the jam pan. Don't worry if a few pips go in the pan.

Stack your skins in piles of four on your chopping board, cut sides upwards. Using a sharp knife, cut in half lengthways, then slice widthways – as chunky or fine as you like. Return the sliced peel to the pan. Add another 1.5 litres of water.

Tie the corners of your muslin together, and submerge the bag in the pan, suspended from the handle. Add any juice that has already run through the muslin. Note the depth of liquid (you can mark on the outside of your jam pan) and bring to a fast boil. Occasionally squeeze the muslin bag against the side of the pan with the back of a wooden spoon to get all the pectin out. Boil to reduce the marmalade by a third (this could take up to an hour).

Take out the muslin pip bag, add your sugar and bring back up to a rolling boil. This is when you need to stir regularly – and carefully! The solids sinking to the bottom of the pan can bubble up like volcanic lava if left too long without stirring.

Boil for 30 minutes to an hour then start testing by placing a few drops onto a cold saucer taken from the fridge. Let the drops cool then run your finger across – if the mixture wrinkles a little then it's ready. It's better underdone than over (you don't want to burn the sugar). You can always cool it and re-boil again.

Ladle marmalade into your clean jars, which don't need to be hot, but don't bring them straight in from a cold storage shed! Put clean sterile lids on when very hot. This gives a good vacuum – you don't need to use wax paper discs.

City farming at Windmill Hill

Neil Kinnock visits the Windmill Hill City Farm, 1983

In 1981 my girlfriend Leslie and I moved to Bristol, where I got the job of farm manager at Windmill Hill City Farm. This amazing city farm project was founded by a group of locals who forged it out of the rubble of a demolished housing estate, creating a vital community and farm hub that remains an ever more important city oasis to this day. Returning today you can see the trees, paddocks and ponds that were put in at least 40 years ago. There were community allotments, a farmyard and mini paddocks, a woodwork shop, a rumpus room and playcentre and a brilliant adventure playground.

The farm was run by a voluntary management committee and had a team of workers paid by various means from local government grants to Youth Training Schemes (YTS), Community Enterprise Project (CEP) and various other government schemes of the time. It was well used by the local community and was a great resource for city wide visitors and school groups.

As farm manager, I worked closely with Simon Phelps who was the community gardens manager. Simon was an inspiration to many, not least because he had to live with being wheelchair bound after an accident in his 20s. This never stopped him from getting on with all garden works. Over the four years I was there, the gardens and the farm were used by all sorts of groups from schoolchildren to patients from Glenside psychiatric hospital. Alongside this were many local children who loved being around the animals on the farm - pigs, goats and especially poultry. Collecting eggs always brings out joy in younger children.

Food production on a city farm

The place was a bit of a pets' corner when I arrived and I wanted to create more of a demonstration farm, showing what food production was all about. To this end we opened a little shop on the farm to sell our produce. Small amounts of vegetables, plenty of eggs of all shapes and sizes including guinea fowl and quail eggs. Of course, we also sold meat from our animals. This was popular especially when we killed a pig and had pork and sausages and it was here that I cured my first rather rustic (and oversalted!) bacon and ham for Christmas. I also made a coarse country style pâté, which was delicious. I used marjoram in the pâté alongside thyme and from this discovery I came to love fresh marjoram in many dishes, from vegetables to poultry to rabbit. It's so easy to grow almost all year round.

There were a number of locals wanting halal meat and they would often arrive wanting to take away a live bird. Instinctively I thought this was fine, but made it clear the bird had to be killed on the farm, so I took part in that with them. It was done with respect and prayer, which is more than is done for most animals.

Roast turkey

Here is a recipe taken from one of our early Better Food newsletters. It's called 'Turkey fit for a king' and was given to us by my brother Barny when he was running the Quartier Vert restaurant.

Ingredients

1 organic bronze turkey,
well hung preferably
For the stuffing
125 g butter
125 g breadcrumbs
1 clove garlic
10 shallots finely diced
125 g streaky bacon finely diced
1 turkey liver finely chopped
zest of 2 lemons
juice of 1 lemon
1 apple finely diced
8 or so fresh sage leaves
finely chopped
1 to 2 teaspoons salt

Method

Melt butter in large pan and sweat off shallots until soft. Add garlic, bacon and apple, stir until lightly caramelised, around 20 minutes or more. Transfer to a bowl and add breadcrumbs, lemon zest and juice, sage, liver and salt. Mix well.

Stuff your turkey and then rub the whole bird well with olive oil and season with salt. Cover it with greaseproof paper and then foil, sealing to the edges of your roasting pan. This can sit like this for a couple of hours if you need to go and open presents!

Place in a preheated oven at 210 deg C for about 20 minutes to get a sizzle seal on your bird.

Turn the heat down to 180 deg C and baste with its juices every 30 minutes until done. Cook for about 15 minutes per kilo plus an additional 30 minutes or so depending on stuffing amounts and the bird's size. Really big birds can take a lot longer. The best way to check if it is done is to use a skewer poked between the leg and breast. If the juice runs out clear it is done, if it is pink, leave it in for longer. If yours weighs over 4 kg, cover it with foil for most of the cooking time and just uncover to brown for the last 20 minutes so it looks the part and your guests can tuck into the skin as well as the flesh.

When it's done remove from its roasting pan into a hot dish. Cover this with foil followed by a tea towel and leave to rest for at least 30 minutes.

Now make your gravy. Place your roasting pan on the stove over a low heat. Stir a little flour into the juices and fat and then add a glass of red wine and some vegetable stock. Season to taste.

If you make sure you have hot plates to serve, hot gravy to add, then the turkey itself only need be warm. And my goodness there is nothing quite like it!

One year we reared some bronze turkeys. Two weeks before Christmas the farm was broken into, the turkeys killed and stolen. It was shocking. All of them had been bashed with a bar the thieves had left behind. Every one of these beautiful birds had been ordered by local people. The story got into the Bristol Evening Post and two days later we had a call from a fish and game merchant in St Nick's market. He had our birds all hanging up like pheasants at the front of his stall. I guess he thought that 20 bronze turkeys on his stall two days after the City Farm had reported theirs stolen could lead to bad press for him. We got them back and had to hang them in a cool place for much too long. They were a bit high by the time they were ready to eat, but absolutely delicious.

Pet food

A year after I started at the farm a local pet shop dropped in 13 fat guinea pigs. Had I been there I would not have taken them, but it was my day off. I made it clear that these lovely creatures would be treated the same as all other farm animals. They were

meat. A week later I set about killing and skinning them. Influenced somewhat by the men who had come to buy halal meat, I paid particular attention to each life I took with a little prayer. 'Bye bye guinea pig, thank you for your gift to our plates.' I had several local children and adolescents with me when I killed the guinea pigs and I talked to them about what I was doing and why. They were all regulars and used to working with me, so were not altogether surprised. While there was laughter and cries of 'How cruel!', they were also very curious. They stayed and watched the whole process including the cutting up of the creatures after skinning and gutting them. One of the YTS farm workers, Alison, decided to become vegetarian, which was a successful outcome in terms of her taking responsibility for what she eats. She had seen it all and made her decision.

After the lives of the guinea pigs were taken for meat, the children returned home and told their families all about it. This started a riot. I got several letters from parents saying I should be sacked, that these were pets and should never be eaten. How could I expose children to such things?

This says a lot about our relationship with food and nature. Our disconnection from food production, particularly in cities, has brought us to buying plastic packs of meat in supermarkets without ever connecting what we are buying with the living animal. In fact, many of those same parents were delighted to be able to buy the farm's meat and were facing up to the reality of meat eating. However, when it came to fluffy creatures like guinea pigs, normally seen as pets, they felt it was cruel to eat them. For a time, I was known as the 'guinea pig killer'.

> ## When you invite good people to join you in action towards a good idea, good things happen

The young people were fine, they understood and learnt so much from the experience. They were forming connections with food and nature and all the activities on the farm were helping them with that. For centuries, guinea pigs have taken a particular place in the family in parts of South America, in the same way that rabbits have been for us. Family pet as well as meat source, they have lived off scraps from the garden and table before becoming a stew for the whole family. The interplay between children's fondness for these animals and safeguarding them as pets only changed as we had access to choice, to wealth and then the resulting disconnection from nature and the source of our food.

Learning to love (and let go) of the animals we eat

Later that year the farm was given a Jersey bull calf. He was such a beautiful creature, with big brown eyes and long eyelashes. We all fell in love with him and there was much cuddling by hundreds of children and a few adults. It was always made clear that, like all the other animals on the farm, he was there in part as food for humans. Jersey calves are known not to be very meaty so there was no point in keeping him too long. Besides he had not been castrated, so at 18 months he was getting quite bull like. It was time for him to go.

Top: Bernie and calf
Bottom: Windmill Hill City Farm

Several customers had asked to order some of his meat. There were also many staff who were ready to sob at the thought of losing him. A few of us spent some time with him saying goodbye and thanking him for all he had done for us, including how much pleasure children had had from stroking him. Two weeks later people were eating him and doing so with a reverence for the life given up for our nourishment. I also cured the hide as best I could - no doubt it still sits on someone's floor today.

The farm was going from strength to strength and by the time I left it had a café, a meat room, a mini shop and a dairy room. We were hatching chicks and rearing them on for meat or eggs. Simon and I planted hedges and trees and created a new paddock over the top of some broken concrete. Over some subsoil we laid a ton or so of mushroom compost into which I sowed a herbal ley.

This paddock is still there today and has goats and other livestock grazing on it. Surrounding the farm are the fruits of the planting, fabulous trees and hedges offering wildlife a sanctuary and a place of natural beauty in the heart of the city. The place is filled with the hubbub of people talking, creating and working to help build a more positive world alongside children having fun and being cared for in ways that they all deserve.

While the farm has faced some tough times over the years and been near to closure on occasion, it is now a bustling thriving city community of happenings. Three cheers for the visionaries that founded such a venture, which could by now be a modern housing estate, perhaps even high rise, with little or no green space.

Vision and teamwork hand in hand

This project provides proof that the best way to make things happen is often to act now and talk later. It takes a certain kind of person with vision and tenacity to launch a project such as this. They may need to be blind to the stepping stones to completion, so that they don't get bogged down in the difficulties, instead offering a creative response to the now, while holding on to the vision.

Looking back, this is also the way I have tackled most of the projects I've been involved with. While I'm proud of the work, it must be said that tears have been shed on the way. People like me tend to leave a trail for others to pick up. It is clear that you need a team of people that recognise the parts they each have to play. While I tend to find certain elements of teamwork hard to accept, I know that when I do, it always leads to the smoother progression of any project.

Right from the start, the founders of the city farm got local people involved. They even got them down to the site to help clear it and with tacit permission from the council made their occupation feel so loved and permanent, they could never get them out. When you invite good people to join you in action towards a good idea, good things happen.

Adventure and food camaraderie on a bike

I t was the year 2000. The Better Food company was going well if, as ever, it was slightly rocky financially and I felt that I needed a distraction. The perfect opportunity came in the form of a sponsored bike ride to raise funds for the Soil Association local food links network. About 20 of us made our way from Bilboa to Barcelona over hills and mountains and down across the plains.

The cycling, the camaraderie and the magnificent countryside made this trip one I shall never forget. The food was good of course, and always welcome, but there was one dish that stood out. Tortilla. The very best example of this was eaten in a house we named Wee Willie Winky, an old rambling mansion that had been owned for many generations by a family who tended a beautiful biodynamic vineyard on the estate. We arrived after a long day of riding, tired and thirsty. After quick glugs of fresh spring water at the farm, we went for something stronger. We were a rowdy, fun-loving bunch and every day ended in much drinking of local wines. That night was no exception, the biodynamic wine flowed and we feasted with the family, tucking into a vast array of delectable home cooked foods. We sat at tables in the dining hall that had to be extended through the hall's double doors and out into the hallway. All the family's wide variety of cutlery and crockery was brought out to sit atop old cotton tablecloths. There was no electricity, so the place was festooned with candles and the odd paraffin lamp, reminding me of Lothlorien.

The tortilla was made by Marianne, the wife of the son who had inherited at least a part share of the vineyard. Marianne did not live at the farm but kept

her own chickens and brought a couple of dozen eggs along. Some thyme from the back of the house, some beautifully waxy potatoes, olive oil, salt, pepper and that was it. It was still warm when we ate it, egg still slightly soft, potatoes cooked through, but still firm and a little oily. The best of the best.

After we had feasted, we all helped wash up by candlelight. Charlie, the tour doctor, played the piano, and we all sang songs finishing the night in high spirits with the help of some local brandy. The next day we set off fresh as daisies, hearts full of the soul of Wee Willie Winky, spirits high and on our way again to Barcelona. Between us we raised many thousands of pounds towards the launch of the Soil Association's local food links work, which was in its infancy at the time but went on to put school food at the heart of public health.

Tortilla

This classic Spanish dish is found in so many good cafés and restaurants and there is fierce competition about what constitutes the authentic and the best. Let's be clear – it was always a frugal, peasant dish that had lots of potatoes, onion and any other veg, cheese or meat scraps. At times it may have been cooked with only 1 or 2 eggs to a kilo of potatoes.

This recipe is a little more generous than that, although still cooked in the traditional way.

Ingredients

600 g peeled waxy potatoes
200 g onion
5 organic eggs
Salt and pepper
Lots of olive oil
And a cupful of love for the chickens who supplied you the eggs.

Method

Slice the potatoes and the onions thinly. Heat a 25 cm frying pan (non-stick does help). Add a small cupful of olive oil.

Add the potato and onion and fry gently until a light golden colour and the potatoes are just cooked. Turn the slices carefully during frying using a spatula to avoid breaking them up too much. The potatoes should have soaked up all the oil. Add a little more if it seems too dry. Take off the heat and cool in a bowl. Add salt and pepper to taste.

Beat the eggs and pour into the bowl and leave these to merge together for an hour or so. It's a great dish to prepare in the afternoon or evening and cook the next day.

Using the same pan, heat some more olive oil and add your egg, potato, and onion mixture. Spread the whole lot out evenly across the pan. It should have eggy mess just topping the whole mix. Cook gently until golden brown underneath and then, using a plate if it's easier, turn and cook the other side. Don't overcook it and keep the heat on the low side.

Serve warm or at room temperature. I like to sprinkle parsley over it or perhaps a little tarragon. It's even better on day 2, eaten at room temperature.

Squash harvest 2012

Community is essential
for our sense of security,
belonging and wellbeing

Community farming

I get excited about visions that are good for humanity and I'm driven to make projects happen. One venture I am very proud to have been a founder of is the building of a community farm in 2009. There was not much that would stop me from jumping hurdles, and enthusing greatly to others to get them on board to ensure this project came to life.

Set in the Chew Valley, 10 miles south of Bristol, the farm overlooks the Chew Valley Lake, a reservoir that was built in the early 1950s to provide for Bristol's expanding demand for water. The farm was to be for the people by the people, growing organic food and trading it. I wanted to show that growing vegetables is good work to be involved in, but importantly that selling it, and doing so profitably, could help support the farm's community work. I hoped people might understand both, and to be part of what had become known as 'community supported agriculture' or CSA. This unique project would therefore put its trade activity at its centre.

Community is essential for our sense of security, belonging and wellbeing. Building communities around food and farming in our fragmented world will always be a huge part of my life's work. As a vision, The Community Farm represented all I had gathered to date from my family life, with the influence of my mum, living in the community of Lothlorien, as well as the experience of growing food and learning about soil health. My business experiences, the job at Windmill Hill City Farm, all combined with my own need to make the world a better place, brought me to this place - a chance to share my skills and knowledge, which by this time were fairly broad and very practical.

A home for a new community

While working at Barley Wood Gardens I had been approached by Luke Hasell and Jim Twine. For many years, Jim's dad, John Twine, had supplied Better Foods with superb yoghurt from his small biodynamic farm of Jersey cows. He had a milk and yoghurt round in Bristol delivering to the Rudolf Steiner school and was well known for natural unpasteurised milk and super creamy yoghurt. This came to an end a year or so before the older Mr Twine died and while the farm no longer had a dairy, Jim took over the care of the land. Luke Hasell was mates with Jim from school days and had also recently lost his Dad who farmed, so had returned to the family farm to take over. Luke and Jim formed a farming partnership and a business called The Story to sell meat. Luke approached me to see if I wanted to grow some vegetables on some of his land. Jim, Luke and I walked the land overlooking the Chew Valley Lake. Wow! It was so beautiful. My head spun with visions of what could become of this place. After some thought, I said I didn't want to tackle this land on my own. It had to be something shared with many. I knew from bitter experience that growing was too much work and you needed 100% commitment or deep pockets to pay others to do it for you. I had neither. However, moving our growing operations from a very poor stony field below the walled gardens to a beautiful site with good deep top soil was hugely tempting, so I went ahead, with the proviso that its future lay as a community project. This would not be just another Phil Haughton enterprise.

In October 2008 Luke sowed an over winter rye and vetch green manure on his 10-acre bottom field for The Better Food Company to benefit from in the

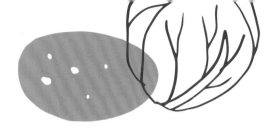

spring of 2009. To get it off the starting blocks, it was down to myself and Atanas, a very strong and trusted right-hand man, who never shied from doing anything. The site was bare – nothing more than a field. Luke offered us a big garden shed/stable that was in an overgrown garden of a house he and his brother owned. Atanas and I set off into the Somerset Levels and dismantled the shed, loading it onto a big flatbed van borrowed from a friend and re-erecting it on the new site as a base for us to store our tools and to shelter in from the rain and cold. We added some basic water piping giving us a tap by the shed. We had built base camp. Next, we got all our kit moved from the old walled garden field site and got on with growing.

That same autumn we planted raspberries, currants and strawberries. They had been so popular at Barley Wood I wanted to establish this as a reliable cash crop that a community farm would benefit from, getting volunteer help to keep up with picking.

In March 2009 Luke spread manure for us and ploughed the field. We took it on from there, preparing soils and planting. Our son Charlie and his friends, freshly out of school and turning 18, earned gap-year travel cash by planting and weeding that spring and summer. I was a hard taskmaster but they rose to the challenge.

From early June onwards, the team had 5 am starts and plenty of weekend work including watering and taking care of the polytunnel temperatures. Our harvested vegetables were loaded into our van and taken into Bristol by 10 am in time for our wholesale rounds and the day's shop customers, not to mention

stocks for our box customers. These harvesting hours were frantic and fun, but you were ready for a coffee by the time the van left.

During the winter of 2009/10 we moved our warehouse operations to the farm buildings close to the field. This would be the new trading heart of what was to become The Community Farm. We had daily harvesting of leeks, greens and much more and at times it was freezing, and on occasion felt like we were in Siberia with no warm place to retreat to. Atanas and I would sometimes wash the leeks to get them ready for the shops and laugh with pain as our fingers began to thaw out after we had finished.

The growing was a huge success that year, producing incredible volumes and variety of fabulous vegetables. I was ambitious in what we produced and exhilarated by this new soil we were working with. I had ordered thousands too many plant plugs, so just

With Luke Hasell and daughter,
planting trees at the Community Farm

had to keep finding space to put them. The land was crammed full of vegetables all summer and autumn. No sooner was one crop out, the next was in. At times we were harvesting in competition with pigeons and deer and we had to learn about covering crops every night before we left. The deer could easily take 150 lettuce in one night, always taking the heart only. We produced over £70,000 worth of vegetables on around 7 acres of ploughed land and one polytunnel that year. This was astonishing for a first full year of growing on a new site.

Moving the vision onward

While all this growing was going on, plans were coming together to form a Community Farm. Luke, Jim and I began talks refining the vision and were ready to engage with others. My wife, Gerry, was the first to join us on our steering group along with Angela Raffle who was working in public health in Bristol, and at the time was involved in Transition Redland. Transition groups grew out of talks and publications by Rob Hopkins. ℝ Several towns started their own groups, to help strengthen communities, respond to environmental issues and look at how together we might respond to climate change. Angela attracted a few other new members including Dave Hunter, a lawyer with his heart and soul embedded in supporting ethical and environmental change. ℝ

Jim hosted a lunch of delicious organic food for a meeting at his farm in Winford, North Somerset, involving all interested parties and we began to work up plans for moving forward. We went on to build a strong group who worked hard to create something really special. The Community Farm was to be a community-owned social enterprise, growing and selling organic food through a box scheme and wholesale delivery service. Its aims were to help people develop a better understanding of where their food comes from, reconnect with the land on which their food is grown, and learn more about sustainable farming, while all the time building community and wellbeing for all.

In 2010 the then steering group was chaired by a good friend Nelisha Wickremasinghe who I knew from her leadership of a Common Purpose course I had attended. The farm steering group were meeting frequently and pushing forward with a plan to deliver this project to be set up through a huge crowdfund.

In 2011 more than 500 people, both local and from around the world, invested in the project with little prospect of a return on their money. There were times when we really thought we would not raise sufficient funds to get it going, but somehow the will to succeed and the increasing support for the idea helped us get enough to launch. The principle behind this project was that the trading activity would be profitable and help support the social

125

investment in community, growing and volunteering activities. To this day, while the trading has been successful, it has never had sufficient funds to fully support the rest of the activities.

There was so much going on in those first years, and all with a sense of pioneering adventure about it; volunteering on the land, school groups, open days, working with people who needed extra support in life for various reasons, and most importantly engaging with the general public.

Community Farmer Days

One of the most popular ways of helping and finding out more was by joining in for a day through what we called Community Farmer Days. On many Saturdays over the year, 10 to 20 people would come to help out and find out about the farm. On these Saturdays there always seemed to be glorious weather. On one such day there was a group of about 10 of us including photographer and volunteer Clare Groom. After working hard in the hot sun, we took to the shade of a big oak tree for a long picnic lunch and talked about what our hopes and aspirations were for The Community Farm. These days buzzed with the emerging spirit of the project. From early on I was aware that we were supporting the community as much as we were being supported by them. One chap who was a little out of sorts with life camped in a small tent at the farm for three months and

volunteered most days. He knew he had friends and food every day and we knew we had someone who would shut down the polytunnel late in the evenings. The farm was a magnet for people seeking community and social support. All we needed was to welcome all and allow enough freedom of use for more vulnerable people to feel safe and not constrained. This experience, like many others in my life, is evidence that good ideas attract good people who in turn make good things happen.

Community Supported Agriculture (CSA)

A board for the farm was now forming and finding its feet in matters of governance. It soon became clear that we needed more support to strengthen our structure and the management of employees. Thankfully there were small grants available at the time for CSA projects such as ours along with some great people who could help to make the project a big success then as it still is to this day. The people working in it and on it, its volunteering activities, its trading management, its board governance, its standing in the community and simply its power for good, is all testament to the work and love so many people have given to ensure its success.

If you have a chance to visit and or support this community farm or any community growing projects near you, I urge you to do so. Projects like this represent one of the most powerful tools for connection and change that exist at this time for all our communities. However small the project, if it is growing food and inviting others to help and take a share of its future then it's a key to helping make the world a better place.

Roasted squash

When I was little no one even knew what a squash was. We had Halloween pumpkins, but that was it. I think my mum started to grow a few in the early 1970s. Certainly, by the time we had a garden at Lothlorien we were growing and eating squashes.

Now they are everywhere and butternut is the biggest seller by far.

Butternut is indeed a great squash, but don't let that limit you from exploring the huge variety that are on offer these days. Box schemes tend to grow small ones that fit the size and value of the box, which may mean box scheme customers are missing a plethora of the larger varieties. So it's the allotment holders who rule the roost for squash varieties. So if you don't grow them, seek out those that do and do a swap of some kind.

Of course, they all behave and taste slightly differently from each other, so no one recipe will fit all.

The great thing with squash is that whatever you do with it, if your recipe hasn't worked well or you have leftovers you can always turn it into soup.

Here is a simple roast recipe inspired by a Jamie Oliver recipe from 2005.

Heat your oven to 180 deg C.

Carefully cut your squash in half, take out the seeds and cut the rest into wedges about 2.5 cm or so across at the widest point leaving the skin on. Put these into a large roasting tin.

Make up a rub with olive oil, salt, pepper, some fresh herbs such as sage, thyme or rosemary chopped roughly and a sprinkle of chilli flakes. Mix together and then rub into the squash. Spread out in the tin with spaces between each wedge so they have a bit of air around them. Jamie suggested you throw in the seeds, but this will depend on how big and tough they are. Try it and see.

Cover the tray with foil and bake for about 20 minutes. Take the foil off and roast off for another 15 or so minutes to get a bit of golden colour.

Try this with a cumin yoghurt dip.

Love, life and community in Abruzzo

Our friends Steve and Marion were looking for volunteers to help with the olive harvest on their little olive grove in Abruzzo. Stephen runs an Italian foodie adventure project in Abruzzo (see resources). For several years Gerry and I had wanted to return to Italy, a country we both love for its culture, its food and its countryside. So we jumped at the chance, knowing it would be hard work in the heat, but rewarding and socially fun. It was also a chance to look for olive oil supplies direct from the producer for our shops. 🅡

The joys of a simple, home-grown feast

While we were there, we were invited to spend a day with the Ferrante family on their farm. Arriving in the yard, we were greeted warmly by Ercolino and his wife Filamina, Elio their son and his wife Sonya as well as several other family and friends. The plan for the day was to have a lesson in making ravioli, then to share what we had made all together and celebrate all that is good about living from the land.

It was a beautiful late October day, warm and sunny but with a cool breeze. Our venue was a big summer kitchen next to a huge lean-to barn under which we would eat. There was a pizza oven fired up, an open fire to warm by in the cool of the stone kitchen, a pasta preparation table and a huge outdoor table to seat 20. Several of us from England helped with pasta making, which was such fun. The women of the house were experts – for them making fresh pasta is just in a normal day's work.

The ravioli were stuffed with a ricotta, egg yolk and Parmesan mixture and served with a simple but delicious tomato sauce. This pomodoro or passata was their own and it had such depth of flavour, you could almost taste the sweet sunshine. This was made three litres at a time and reduced with some bone stock for an hour or more. The recipe took the humble tomato to heavenly heights. The sauce needed no herbs or spices. The cooks are happy to just let the tomatoes sing and indeed this sauce sang to all our hearts' delight.

The meal was long and had many courses. Fracchiata was the first, a mixture of polenta and chickpea flour to which was added a dish they made earlier of garlic, sausage meat, onion, carrot and small chunks of pancetta cooked slowly in plenty of olive oil. The result was a simple thick soupy dish topped with flakes of dried sweet Romano red peppers that were fried in oil to a crisp. So simple and yet a perfect autumn dish. Then fresh borlotti beans cooked in pumpkin, again cooked for hours with the beans and pumpkin making great bedfellows. A soft, earthy, slightly sweet experience that demanded to be tried at home - the children loved it. None of this was gourmet fare, just traditional Abruzzo family food.

Next came the ravioli. Lovingly made using 00 flour, this was the dish of the day and it was complemented beautifully by that gorgeous tomato sauce.

This was followed by roast cockerel cooked in the pizza oven. The oven was fired up first with old olive tree prunings, followed by the very same tree's logged branches and it didn't take much to reach the heat required. Once the stone was heated right through to Ercolino's satisfaction the fire was mostly swept out to make way for the chicken pieces in a heavy roasting

Filamina and Ercolino Ferrante

129

Elio Ferrante

barbecue made to take the skewers. The lamb – their own of course – needed little seasoning other than a big sprinkle of salt while cooking. In fact, everything we ate was from the farm, each course small and simple in style, but with so much time, love and care going into the making of it. All this washed down with local red wine and finished off with local ice cream, an expresso and a grappa for those who could not resist. The hospitality offered was overwhelming in its generosity and warmth. There were at least six of us at their table they had never met. It was their love of Steve and Marion that brought us all together.

pan. It cooked fast, while a sweating Ercolino turned and moved it around with a paddle. Finally, removed from the oven and left on hot stones for 20 minutes or so, we ate it. It tasted divine, with a robust earthy flavour, crispy skin and smoky edges. This bird had been running around the farmyard waking everyone at dawn only a day or so before. Ercolino smiled proudly. His cockerel had been reared from the egg and was now a precious gift to our table.

The last main course was extraordinary. Arrosticini (lamb brochettes), cooked on a specially long

Quality and abundance for healthy living

Elio and his family live off the land, with olive oil being the main harvest and their income source. Alongside this they bottle the fabulous passata. They use a lot at home and the rest is for sale, a truly handmade product. With the help of Stephen's fluent Italian, Elio and his father and I talked about olive oil and passata for the Better Food shops. This family produce simple good food and they expect no more than a modest return. In the UK, we are used to buying the bargain olive oil and tinned tomatoes from industrial scale producers. We wondered if we really would be able to provide a good market for these lovely people? Yes, of course we could! Better Food can and must sell these wonderful organically produced foods. This is partly what our job is, to open markets for the best producers and celebrate those who grow with respect for the land wherever they are.

In Italy, they use excellent quality oil for everything in lavish abundance – it is part of their daily healthy diet. In the UK, we seem to think we must use cheap oil for

The hospitality offered was overwhelming in its generosity and warmth

Polenta on the table with sausages or mushroom in a tomato sauce

The cooks Teresa Foschini and Filomena Marrone offer this recipe

Polenta is an autumn and winter dish, typical of the northern and central regions of Italy.

Preparing it is simple but in addition to the basic ingredients in the right proportions, you will need time and a lot of patience: the polenta must cook slowly, possibly in a copper pot or in a thick-bottomed non-stick saucepan. The secret to obtaining a homogeneous, lump-free mixture is to mix the dough throughout the cooking time, remembering that the more the polenta cooks, the tastier and more digestible it will be.

The proportions of water and polenta are important for the preparation of this dish. For 4 people 250 g of polenta are needed with 1.5 litres water.

Method

Bring the water to a boil with a little salt. As soon as the water starts to boil, add the polenta by sprinkling it in, little by little, vigorously beating with a whisk during the first minutes of cooking to dissolve the lumps. Then lower the heat to the minimum and cook the polenta without ever stopping stirring, always in the same direction, with a long-handled wooden spoon, so that the mixture does not stick to the bottom of the pot.

Cook it for about 30-50 minutes. It should come away from sides of the pan, and be able to support a spoon. The polenta is ready.

If the polenta dries out too much you can add a ladle of slightly salted boiling water. If, on the other hand, it is too soft, leave it on the heat for a few more minutes.

Once cooked, pour the polenta onto a wooden table where you will eat it if you choose to do so in the Abruzzo tradition, or, if you prefer, use a tray lined with greaseproof paper.

Pour over the polenta a good, well-seasoned tomato sauce containing pork sausage meat or mushrooms. Add cheese if you want the cherry on top!

Enjoy!

Ravioli (con sugo)

Serves 4

Tomato ravioli are a delight, much loved by both adults and children.

For the sugo (tomato sauce)

1 large onion
300 ml tomato passata
herbs, salt, pepper to season
Grated parmesan to taste
Extra virgin olive oil

Preparation of the sugo

Peel the onion, slice it and put in a pan with two tablespoons of olive oil. When the onion is soft add the tomato passata, salt, pepper and herbs. Stir and cook over low heat for 15 to 20 minutes.

Meanwhile, heat a pot full of salted water and add the ravioli when it starts to boil. Cook them al dente, then drain and add them to the pan with the tomato sauce. Sprinkle with grated Parmesan.

For the ravioli

4 eggs
400 g of 00 flour

To make the fresh pasta, pour 400 g of flour (keeping some aside to add if necessary) onto a wooden pastry board. Create a recess in the centre and add the whole eggs, then mix with the fork and at the same time begin to incorporate the flour, bit by bit.

Once the liquid has been absorbed into the flour, start kneading by hand using your palm, for about 10 minutes. Vigorously pull it in all directions until the dough is smooth. Let it rest at room temperature for at least 30 minutes (covered with a tea towel). Once rested, cut a piece of dough, flour it and put it through the dough roller of a pasta machine set to the maximum thickness. Pass the dough between the rollers to obtain a first sheet which will be thick. Fold the two edges of the sheet towards the centre, sprinkle again with a very small amount of flour and pass it again between the rollers. Once a rectangular sheet is obtained, lay it on the lightly floured surface and trim the ends with a knife. Divide it into two parts and pass each one through the rollers again and again, adjusting the machine each time until you have reached the thinnest setting. At this point your fresh egg pasta is ready.

A thin sheet of egg pasta, smooth and homogeneous, is one of the secrets for obtaining perfect homemade ravioli.

Our ravioli are half-moon shaped and stuffed with cow's milk ricotta and Abruzzese rigatino cheese (a seasoned sheep's cheese with a very delicate flavour).

Place small amounts of the filling the size of a hazelnut at regular intervals onto the rolled-out dough. Cut the pasta into circular shapes with the filling in the centre. Fold the circles with your fingers and as you do, press the pasta all around well, letting the air out. In this way, you reduce the risk of the ravioli swelling and breaking while cooking, letting the filling leak out.

Making ravioli for
the community feast

cooking and keep the good stuff to be used sparingly for salads. It's like using really cheap nasty wine for cooking. All good chefs will use at least decent quality wine and oils for cooking. I reckon on using about a litre a month for the two of us at home. That's less than 50p a day and a very good investment it is for health, and for the love of life.

The Ferrantes bring the feast to Bristol

In Nov 2018 the Ferrante family came over to Bristol to help us celebrate the introduction of their olive oil into our stores. We had chosen our new store down by the harbour to host the evening feast. The Ferrantes were determined to cook all of it themselves, with Lewis our catering manager on hand to support them.

The evening was like a crazy Haughton family supper in that we were tight for space on a long table and elbows had to be kept firmly under control. And there were many voices competing to be heard. It was noisy, exuberant, colourful and with wine flowing freely.

Several small dishes were served to start. After these were dispatched, all guests had to stand and move away, drinks in hand and much to chatter about, while we cleared the table for the show-stopping dish to come. 'Polenta on the table', a dish most Brits will be unlikely to have experienced the like of. Using one of Italy's staple foods, polenta, this dish would traditionally have been served with whatever was available from the garden or farm. The family would gather for the main meal and eat from the table, with each person, spoon in hand, carving out their own area to eat. See recipe on page 131.

This, served at Better Food in Wapping Wharf, was a sight to behold! Once everyone was re-seated and tucking into the feast laid out on the 60-foot table, it was clear that this was a great way to celebrate simple food with a group of family and friends.

We finished the meal off with an almond cake, with ricotta and Campari sauce made by Lewis our chef. A good night was had by all and I hope the Ferrante family will never forget the way the English can celebrate when they put their minds to it.

Community building around food

Community kitchen activities are increasing all over the world, whether that be in the form of cookery schools, shared cooking spaces, community meals and many other ventures. What they all have in common is that they are connecting people with each other and creating community through a common language of generosity, sharing and celebration of food.

My brother Barny and I have always had a strong connection through our love of food and farming. In fact, when researching for this book I found an article in an old *Venue* magazine about the three Bristol Haughtons, Barny, Liz and myself, and the work we were all doing in food. This was when Barny had just started a restaurant called Bordeaux Quay. He went on several years later to create The Square Food Foundation, a charity teaching people from all walks of life to cook, to appreciate and to love the food they cooked from scratch.

Located in Knowle West in Bristol, a tough estate with a history of deprivation, this was not a place with much food culture. From day one, Square Food operated on a not-for-profit basis. Square Food masterclasses and private events subsidised work with schools and community groups. It's a cookery school that delivers so much more than classes. It is full of passion and hospitality, giving people from all walks of life more confidence in working with raw ingredients while having fun and building community at the same time.

In 2017 Square Food launched a great project in partnership with a Bristol homeless charity St Mungo's, called Streets to Kitchen. Better Food pledged to raise £10k through sponsored events. Some products purchased meant a £1 of every sale went to support this amazing project, which we see as a vital part of revitalising and connecting individuals and communities with mainstream business. Part of being a responsible business means taking our social and community roles seriously. We are all in this together. Connecting up with such projects could be the norm for all business if we choose a compassionate approach to culture and our place within our communities.

Nathalie Moukarzel and Meg Doherty
Cofounders of Fat Macy's

Community has always been at the heart of Fat Macy's. The very foundation of what we do lies in people coming together to create and produce the most fundamental enjoyment in life: food. We create a sense of togetherness as we bake and cook in the kitchen - working alongside one another and sharing stories. Cooking creates a true sense of community. As we share recipes and the stories behind them, we get to know each other better. Trainees often come to us with their grandmother's recipe for the best jerk chicken, or an incredible shakshuka that they want to recreate. Whether likeminded or not, this communal activity connects us in ways that last beyond the food that we cook together.

We are a social enterprise making life-changing food. Using seasonal ingredients, our team are made up of young Londoners, supported on their journey from hostels to their own homes. Trained by our talented chefs and mentors, they add their own stories to create a unique dining experience.

At Fat Macy's we have found that there is something simply beautiful in learning a recipe together, or tasting the fruits of our labour at the end of a long shift. It is nothing short of gratifying to be able to share our work with people through the Fat Macy's Supper Clubs and events.

During every step of what we do, Fat Macy's is here to enable our trainees to realise their true potential and know that they are part of a community; not just at Fat Macy's but community everywhere. Food unites us all, through colour, smell, taste and touch. It brings us together and creates a sense of equality when sometimes spirits waiver.

Fat Macy's is and always has been a place where we cook our meals together, set our table together, enjoy our food together, and then share what we have learnt, meaning that when our trainees make their individual journeys from hostel to home, they do it knowing that they are not alone.

Top: Meg Doherty
Bottom: Nathalie Moukarzel

Fat Macy's Mezze

Feeds 4-6

Labneh

500 g yoghurt will yield 250 g labneh add ¼ teaspoon salt for each 100 g of yoghurt

Season full-fat yoghurt with salt, then strain through a muslin or dishcloth for 24–48 hours.

Smoked paprika hummus

200 g chickpeas (cooked)
3 tablespoons tahini
½ teaspoon sea salt
1 teaspoon smoked paprika
1 large clove garlic
4 tablespoons water
3 tablespoons lemon juice

Juice the lemons. Blend all the ingredients together using either a food processor, jug blender or hand blender – until creamy and smooth. You can eat this right away, although it works best when chilled first. Serve with pitta bread, crackers or with salad.

Fatayer

Dough:
½ tablespoon active dry yeast
100 ml lukewarm (40 deg C) water
190 g all purpose or 00 flour
130 g all purpose or pastry flour
½ tablespoon sugar
½ tablespoon salt
40 ml olive oil

Filling:
450 g spinach
2 medium onions
2 tablespoons sumac
½ tablespoon salt
½ teaspoon paprika
¼ teaspoon black pepper
pinch cayenne pepper
2 tablespoons pine nuts (optional)

Dressing:
¼ cup lemon juice
¼ cup extra virgin olive oil
1–2 tablespoons pomegranate molasses (optional)

In a small bowl, sprinkle yeast over the water. Let sit for a minute before stirring to combine. Let sit again until frothy (about 10 minutes).

If you have a food processor with a dough hook, lucky you, place the dry ingredients together and follow the steps below. If you don't, combine flour, salt and sugar in a large bowl and mix with a wooden spoon.

Gradually stir in the oil, then the yeast with water until the dough comes together. On a lightly greased surface, knead until smooth and elastic. Place in large bowl, cover, and let rest for 1–2 hours.

136

If using fresh spinach, place a large pan over medium heat and drizzle with about 1 tablespoon olive oil. Add spinach and cook just until wilted. Remove to a colander. Once cool enough to handle, squeeze out all excess moisture. For frozen spinach, defrost and squeeze out all excess moisture.

Finely chop the onions and place in a medium bowl. Stir in the sumac, salt, paprika, black pepper and cayenne. Let sit while you make the dressing.

In a small bowl, combine lemon juice, olive oil, and pomegranate molasses, if using. Set aside.

Squeeze all excess moisture from the onions. Combine the onions and pine nuts with the spinach. Lightly coat with the dressing until just moistened, not wet.

Preheat oven to 180 deg C. Line two baking sheets with parchment or lightly grease.

Divide the dough in half, placing one of the halves to one side under a cover. On a large, oiled work surface, roll the dough until thin, 1–2 mm. Use a 10 cm circle cutter to cut out the dough.

Place about 1 tablespoon filling in the centre of each circle. Pinch together three edges of the circle over the centre of the filling. Seal down one side, then across the other to form pyramid shape. Place on prepared baking sheet and repeat with remaining circles and other half of dough.

Bake in preheated oven until golden, 15–20 minutes. Let cool slightly before serving.

Tabbouleh

50 g bulgur wheat
50 g flat-leaf parsley, chopped
50 g mint, chopped
200 g ripe tomatoes, deseeded and diced
3 spring onions, finely sliced
juice 1 lemon
3 tablespoons olive oil

Rinse the bulgur wheat in a sieve until the water runs clear. Drain and transfer to a bowl. Pour over 200 ml boiling water, cover with cling film and leave to soak for 30 minutes.

Keeping the parsley in a bunch, chop the leaves roughly. Don't worry about the inclusion of some of the stalks; this all adds to the flavour. Now do the same with the mint. Put the chopped herbs in a large bowl and add the tomato and spring onion.

Thoroughly drain the bulgur, then add to the herb mix, along with lemon juice and olive oil. Mix thoroughly, season and serve.

Resources
Better community

Organisations for better community

Community Supported Agriculture
https://communitysupported
agriculture.org.uk/

The Community Farm,
Chew Magna, Somerset
www.thecommunityfarm.co.uk/

Transition Network
A movement of communities
coming together to reimagine
and rebuild our world
transitionnetwork.org

Books

Hopkins, Rob (2008) *The Transition Handbook: From oil dependency to local resilience*, Green Books.

Hopkins, Rob (2011) *The Transition Companion: Making your community more resilient in uncertain times*, Transition Books

Pinkerton, Tamzin & Hopkins, Rob (2009) *Local Food: How to make it happen in your community: How to unleash a food revolution where you live*, Transition Books

Articles, blogs, web

Italian Culinary Adventure
https://www.casadelcolle.co.uk/
culinary-adventure

Stuart, Graeme (2013) '10 things I've learnt about strengths-based community engagement', Sustaining Community, sustainingcommunity.
wordpress.com/2013/10/31/
strengths-based-ce (accessed 11 June 2020)

Through colour, smell, taste and touch, food brings us together and creates a sense of equality when sometimes spirits waiver

Better business

Finding new ways to put people and planet before profit

Our world is led by an outdated, exploitative capitalist approach to doing business. Now is our time for change. The shareholder model based on returning maximum profit will not be given up lightly, so change will be slow and painful, but change we must. The evidence has permeated every corner of our planet. This model is at the heart of the degradation of nature and climate. All people on earth are suffering including those receiving the financial rewards. Far from being rewarding, this system alienates the rich often leaving them lonely and afraid. This in turn creates entrenchment and wall building, which often lead to warfare. Our best hope for change in business is to move beyond anger to compassion and an invitation to be part of community. When a financially wealthy person gets their hands in the soil it tells them like no other element on earth that we are all the same and money is no protection for a shared world.

The top principle of better business is surely about putting people first, then planet and finally profit. For me, the founding cornerstone of my business is trust, respect and care of everyone involved: those we employ, those who supply us and those we serve.

My 40 years in business have always been mission led, with people and planet as my priorities. Despite this, the pressure of having to play the money game has been stressful and beyond tough at times. Perhaps the very best we can do is to develop a mindful approach to business. Creating profitable businesses may still be necessary in this world of ours, but we don't have to do it at the expense of our humanity or the planet that hosts us.

Phil talked to...
Jamie Hartzell

Jamie is one of the UK's leading social entrepreneurs. He is currently co-chair of CAG Oxfordshire, chair of the Real Farming Trust, and a director of Positive Money, the Sustainable Restaurant Association and of the Ethical Property Company. He is also working hard to double tree cover in Oxfordshire as a response to climate change.

© mimsaxl

Phil: Tell me what's important to you about ethical business?

Jamie: Business shapes the world. It provides the goods and services we need, in the most efficient way possible. At the same time, it can be highly destructive, mistreating workers, consuming resources and generating waste and pollution, with the cost of clean-up falling to the public purse.

Ethical business, in which financial, social and environmental gains are all maximised is a win-win. It generates wealth at the same time as being good for society and the environment. It's a virtual circle – the more money the business makes the better. The time for ethical business has come. Indeed, it has to, as our problems are now so pressing that without it civilisation stands little chance.

Phil: Do you have any suggestions for people as to how they can do/act/work to make change in the business world?

Jamie: Believe that you can bring about change. It can often feel that nothing you do makes a difference. But it does. Shop with your values in mind, and you help to influence others. Speak to your MP and councillor and they will, at least to some extent, listen.

And the more you do this, the better you get at it and the more influence you will have.

Phil: What do our leaders and governors need to do most to help make change?

Jamie: They need to find a way to run the world that is not centred around growth and GNP. GNP is no longer, indeed never has been, a measure of what is important. Spending time looking after children or an elderly relative are not counted in GNP as they are not paid work. On the other hand, prostitution and illegal drugs trading is! Growth is destructive to the environment, generates inequality and is ultimately unsustainable. We need to start making decisions on the basis of the things that really matter like health and wellbeing. But to achieve this is going to require a massive paradigm shift and some very brave leaders!

Dandelion petal jelly

I just made dandelion petal jelly for the first time. We have so many in our garden, I didn't want them to seed, nor to waste them. It's incredibly easy to make and tastes like runny honey!

Ingredients

100 g very fresh dandelion blossoms
800 ml water
800 g sugar (don't use less)
2 tablespoons lemon juice
1 drop yellow food colouring if desired
(without this colouring it's a bit greenish)

Method

Pull the yellow blossom out of the tiny green leaves. Remove as much of the green as possible because it will colour the jelly and make it bitter.

In a saucepan, bring water to a boil. Add the blossoms, stir and cover for 1 to 2 minutes on a low simmer. Turn off water and steep for 20 minutes. Using a muslin or fine mesh strainer, strain out and gently press the blossoms to remove some of the water.

Measure steeping liquid to 3 cups; add sugar, lemon juice and (optional) food colouring and bring to a boil, stirring until sugar dissolves. Boil for 1 minute, then skim off any foam with a wooden spoon.

Pour into hot, sterilised, half-pint (300 ml) jars leaving 6 mm headspace and store in the refrigerator.

Real Food Supplies

In 1984 I began my journey as an entrepreneur. My girlfriend Leslie and I were living in Kingston Road in Southville, Bristol and I took over a side room as a base for a home delivery business. I felt a strong need to trade in organic food in a way that honoured the farmer and the soil as well as celebrating the wonder of the food they produced. I had learnt from my times in community living and farming, I had loved city farming and now it was time to try my hand at retail.

I was very passionate about the subject of organic food and farming. I wrote crazy newsletters, typed and then printed on an old Gestetner stencil machine. I campaigned for organic farming versus chemical farming and against supermarkets in favour of small independents. In 1985 I opened a shop on Gloucester Road called Real Food Supplies. It was the first one-stop organic shop outside London, stocking nothing but good wholesome, organic food, no ready meals or convenience foods.

Real food from real people and real places

The provenance of the food and the farms it came from was all important to me and I was driving all over the country. I'd be picking up cheese from the Deauvilles in Staffordshire, organic vegetables from a warehouse in Yeovil, more vegetables from Flax Drayton farm, run by Francis and John Blake. I made trips to a small sheep farm near Winford in the Quantocks, and long journeys across Wales to seek out fabulous cheeses, like Pantyllyn and Colby. The shop looked great, crammed as it was with home-made rope shelves along the walls framed by the loveliest stencilling done by Leslie. Wooden benches below held more produce and behind a deli counter filled with cheeses, meats and homemade tofu were organic wines from Vintage Roots, a start-up organic wine importing business.

People would turn up at the store to tell me about products they were making and if they were organic and local I took them. One woman from Glastonbury appeared one day with a snack bar she was making out of raw nuts and dried fruit with carob and ginger under the name Ploughshare. It is still going to this day, very handmade, very little packaging and still being stocked at our Better Food shops. They remain small and simple, and still produce fabulous, nutritious, organic food at its best.

I was riding high, moving fast and furiously with a passion for what I was creating with a constant demand for what I was building and much delight from suppliers who were at last finding a market that really constituted best practice in selling organic food. Real Food Supplies quickly became a bustling community store meeting local needs for organic foods.

I campaigned for organic farming versus chemical farming and against supermarkets in favour of small independents

One of our most local suppliers was a woman in St Pauls who made fabulous fresh tofu for us in her kitchen while looking after a small brood of children. We were able to barter a bit as she ordered boxes of organic food for the family, so I delivered to her and picked up super fresh organic tofu to sell in the shop at the same time.

The Real Food Supplies mission 1986

This mission was beautifully handwritten by a friend Eliza, framed and was clearly visible on the wall by anyone entering our store.

Over the past 40 years a growing number of farmers have become aware of the consequences of modern farming methods. The constant pouring on of chemicals and highly intensive animal rearing have led to depletion of the top soil, and major health problems in stock and the food they provide. This concern among farmers has been matched in recent years by demand from the consumer for healthier, better tasting food; the production of which is environmentally safe and respects animal welfare.

Worldwide, there is growing awareness that we can no longer afford to ignore the extent to which we have abused our planet, not only on our farms, but also by the destruction of the rain forests, the over use of cars, and the many forms of industrial pollution currently choking the earth.

Organic farming is a natural approach to agriculture using sound rotations and healthy stock to build soil fertility, and produce food packed with flavour and vitality.

People's concern for the environment and the health of our children is no longer being ignored. Many politicians now see the need for change, and the media has put food and its production in everyone's minds. Organic farming is proving to be an economically viable alternative to chemical agriculture.

Real Food Supplies is here to provide a link between your demand for organic food and the farmers and growers producing it. We aim to stock the greatest possible variety of produce, which meets the standards of the Soil Association, who have for 40 years been campaigning for changes to our agricultural methods, and now provide a comprehensive set of organic standards recognised throughout Europe. Our range of food includes fruit and vegetables, cheese and wine, dry foods and a large range of fresh meat. As well as food we stock a range of organic gardening supplies and ecologically sound cleaning products: all this makes us one of the very few one-stop organic shops.

The one-stop organic shop in the South West

Eighteen months after opening, I knocked a doorway through a thick stone wall and took over the shop next door. By now we had a full-scale organic butchers, a larger grocery, fresh produce and deli store, plus an organic and environmental garden and wildlife section upstairs.

There was increasing demand in the butcher's store and I was making huge quantities of my own recipe sausages every week. Lamb, red wine, coriander and garlic; pork, sweet pepper and honey; a fabulous cooking chorizo; and a spectacular beef merguez. People just could not get enough of them, especially in BBQ season. The thing about a small butcher's store is you are only as good as your butcher. Dave the butcher went sick one Friday evening and I went in at 5 am on Saturday to get the butcher's store ready. I had to cut up a whole hind quarter of beef! That's all the expensive bits and you can't afford to get it wrong. I had never done it before, but I had seen it done and had a reasonable idea of what came from where. Somehow by 9 am I was almost done and the counter was full. The sirloin, the rump, the fillet were all fine, the topside and silverside rolling was a bit marginal, but the show went on and all were happy. I was shattered but thankful that the next day was Sunday and in those days we closed on Sundays.

Rocinantes

I n 1988, my brother Barny opened a landmark business - Rocinantes tapas bar on Whiteladies Road. Not only did Barny produce the sort of tapas dishes the UK had never experienced, but he also committed to doing a fair bit of it using organic produce. Real Food Supplies were fortunate to be their organic supplier. This gave Barny and me a chance to have both a trade and a brotherly relationship, which was strong, rich and at times a bit stormy. No restaurant outside London was using so much organic food. This was real pioneering stuff and the BBC employees down the road loved it. There were some summer days when the place would be rammed from lunch until midnight serving up thousands of little dishes.

Rocinantes made history and Barny earned his place internationally as a great chef who ensured his food was not just superb to eat, but ethical and organic to boot. Barny was always a brother I looked up to, he was the one who had looked out for me most when I was young and I was deeply proud to be supplying him and very pleased that he wanted to support me in what I was doing. We have gone on to work together further, sharing our passion for justice, both social and environmental, in food and farming to this day.

Family eating outside Rocinantes, 1989

148

Raymond Blanc

In 1998, Better Food won the Soil Association Vegetable Box of the Year Award. This prestigious annual industry award made our team very proud. These awards included some well-known judges including Raymond Blanc who judged the meats. One year, Better Food had the job of getting several farmers' meat packs to him at his restaurant, Le Manoir au Quat'Saisons. The job fell to me and my 11-year-old stepson Ed came along with me. At about 8 pm we set off for Oxford.

We were warmly welcomed by Raymond himself at the back door of the kitchens. He brought us into the main part of the huge kitchens. The first thing I noticed were six massive trays of beef bones cooling off after having been roasted in the ovens. This is how great chefs make gravy. Once roasted they were put into vast stock pots and boiled up with onions, carrots, bay leaf, celery, and many other things.

Service had finished a short while before we arrived, so there were some chefs purposefully cleaning down like beavers sweeping their dams. Before we left, Raymond proudly showed us the patisserie. Our jaws dropped and we grinned from ear to ear. This was

The detail that went into these handmade chocolates was unlike anything I have ever seen

a place of such fine work. The detail that went into these handmade chocolates and mini gateaux was unlike anything I have ever seen. Each one a picture of perfect colour combinations, shining with icing decoration, precise and delicate. Frankly, I would never have thought to actually eat them - rather you might frame them and stare endlessly at their perfection and beauty. Lastly, and most impressively, the petits fours. There was an array of mini treats – crunchy ones, swirly ones, spongy ones, iced ones, flaky ones, you name it they were all there. Raymond took out a little box, laid a napkin in its bottom and filled it with about a half a dozen of these petits fours for Ed and me to eat on our journey back home. It was a memorable trip indeed thanks to Raymond's warm hospitality and his gratitude that we had travelled late into the night to take him the food he would judge for the awards. We arrived home after midnight, Ed fast asleep for most of the journey. He had eaten just a couple of Raymond's treats, saving some to give to his Mum and tell her the story of our adventure.

A farmers' market for Bristol

Bristol's fish market in St Nick's at the centre of the city had gradually lost its traders over the span of a generation. It's a beautiful building that belonged to the council and in 1988, as it lay empty, I approached the council about creating a farmers' market. This was to turn into a pilot of the new generation of farmers' markets, many of which thrive to this day. We had a lot of fun with this. Stall holders included vegetable growers, Ian Pardoe the apple grower, a beef farmer from Somerset, yoghurt and raw milk by John Twine, a salmon and trout smoker, as well as some fresh trout from Chew Valley Lake. And one of the last small watercress growers, John Hurd, who had superb bunches of watercress (zero plastic, just ice to keep it fresh).

Farmers' markets were soon to become part of the UK landscape offering a direct connection between producer and consumer and a superb chance to hear the story behind the food. This was the first meaningful fight back for small producers against the supermarket monopoly. Producers make a living from the markets because they have no middle trader to support.

These markets now exist all over our country and are generally thriving. While they represent a tiny percentage of the nation's food purchasing, they are culturally significant and accessible to people from many walks of life. We would do well to keep supporting them.

Charlie, aged two, 'helping' pack veg boxes

Creating a new trading campaign

Sadly, Real Food Supplies had to close early in 1990. Interest rates at 15% and heavy borrowing left me no choice. It was a sad day after five years of organic trading and growing the Bristol organic retail market from almost zero.

In 1989 I had met and fallen in love with Gerry and in May 1991 our son Charlie was born. We married in 1992 and had a beautiful and spirited wedding party. My brother Barny did the food and wine out of his Rocinantes kitchen. He and his chefs came along and set up a huge barbecue under a rough canvas canopy offering us sardines fresh from Brixham markets, and lamb brochettes alongside vibrant tasty salads. A dear friend Gaye and my brother Luke did our cake - a profiterole pyramid with spun sugar brittle cascading over it. It was a wonderful celebration with all our family and friends sharing the day.

Bankruptcy done with and wounds licked, I was never going to stand still for long, it was just not in my nature, and anyway I had to earn some money. I was ready to set about starting a new business, learning the lessons of my past. It was time to get more serious about pushing back at the supermarkets and at chemical farming. I just hated sitting on the side lines letting them have it all their own way and seemingly hoodwinking most consumers and indeed growers to believe they had all the answers and that the food industry was safe with them. I began by using my old contacts and started to deliver some vegetable boxes, milk, eggs and meat.

By the time Charlie was two there were days when he was helping to put vegetables in the boxes. It was a small start with nothing other than a van and £600

to get me launched, but my sights were set higher this time. I was determined to make it bloody well work this time if it killed me!

It felt like a real privilege to be living and working at home with my son who was able to see and take part in my work life. The more we can allow children into our work lives the better it is, so they can grow up with a sense of what it is to work. The relationship we have with our children is not only about provision of love and care, but also provision of insight and learnings.

I was determined to ensure this new venture was secure and well controlled. Every week I did my accounts to ensure it was working well. Phil's Better Food Campaign grew fast, supported by Gerry working as a teacher with a real salary. On a Tuesday we would sit in bed late at night with my book of handwritten orders, extracting all the components using five-bar gates to count the yoghurts and pints of milk that people either picked up from our house at given times, or were delivered. With all the ordering, picking up from suppliers, making up orders, and delivering, it was not long before I was again working long hours. Our back kitchen and old lean-to bathroom were full of boxes and sacks. Much of the box packing had to be done outside in the back garden while on a Wednesday and Thursday, the main kitchen and hallway, were full of orders waiting to be delivered or to be collected. Our house was rammed with freezers full of meat, shelves stacked with wholefoods, and fridges full of milk and yoghurt.

After a year of trading from home, I took on more help and we moved to a Victorian stable block in a back

Family getting married!

lane of Cotham called Gibson Road. It was a two-storey building, cold, damp, and musty in winter, hot and airless in summer. I bought an old refrigerated van and kept it on the road using it as a cold store, only to find it had disappeared one morning. As it had no tax or insurance I thought it best not to bother reporting it to the police.

The only improvement we made to the building was to install a proper loo. I had a dear friend and builder who was installing a flash new bedroom and bathroom for Raymond Blanc, so we got his old green loo and wooden loo roll holder. The holder is to this day in our house in Regil in Somerset.

For a few days a week I began to employ several people who were, it has to be said, prepared to put up with rather poor working conditions. I was so used to roughing it, I really wasn't aware that this was far from ideal. Over the next few years we grew and moved, grew more and moved again until we were in a large warehouse in the Bristol neighbourhood of St Werburghs where more and more people were helping us to keep pace with the growth. Gerry would arrive twice a week from school during her lunch break and do all the invoicing with pen and calculator. A team of drivers used their own cars and vans to do deliveries, which by now were stretching as far as 25 miles from base. Trying to find houses in the dark in the winter, long before satnav or mobile phones, led to some deciding it was not for them, while others stayed with us for many years and were so generous with their energy and commitment. We were all passionate about making organic food available to more and more people. To this day that remains the case at Better Food.

With so many others involved in the campaign, it was time to change the name from Phil's Better Food Campaign to The Better Food Campaign. Our core business was still a wide variety of fruit and veg boxes. The most popular box that continues to this day under the umbrella of The Community Farm, was the Family Provider, designed to keep an average family going for the week with its staples and a bit more. So the usual potatoes, carrots, onions and greens but then more seasonal vegetables like courgettes and tomatoes in summer, or mushrooms and swede in winter. The fruit was again seasonal: apples, pears, plus imported items like bananas and oranges, with clementines in abundance at Christmas time.

The big move

In 2001 The Better Food Campaign moved to The Bristol Proving House in St Werburghs, a 1970s-built warehouse and showroom that had been empty for 15 years. Keen to move more into retail, I was inspired and excited by this whole building, which was on the market at £500k.

I put together a vision for an Ethical Trading Centre. The Centre would be full of community activity: bike workshops, community publishing, crafts workshops and of course our very own organic shop. After much discussion with architects and local supporters we heard that Scrapstore, a charity helping to turn waste into playthings, were also keen on the space, so Better Food and Scrapstore teamed up. Scrapstore bought the building and we moved in as their tenants.

This was our new home from which we did home delivery. We also opened a shop for three days a week and ran our wholesale operation, serving among others a Steiner school called St Christopher's and my brother's restaurant, Quartier Vert, from the warehouse.

Home delivery was becoming increasingly challenging to make financially viable. The cost of moving too had put a great deal of pressure on the business. So I took the huge decision of dropping

Cheap food is in fact expensive. Good food is the right price.

home delivery and opening the shop six days a week. This gave us a chance to focus on building a community store serving the local people with great organic food. Having taken this leap, I realised that face-to-face retail was the way forward for me. It represented the best way to connect with customers and tell the stories of our farmers and producers, even opening up the opportunity to bring them into the store to talk directly with those buying their products.

This area of St Werburghs, close to the start of the M32 motorway, was run down and provided hideaway places for drug dealing and prostitution to grow. We would make it a daily chore to go around the site and pick up needles, durex and other unsavoury detritus. Yet, just by opening our doors on this street people felt safer. When you show a willingness to care and to offer people some nourishing foods, changes begin to happen. The drug and prostitution in the area reduced year on year, unfortunately simply moving to new places.

Organic food doesn't cost the earth

The first few years were tough financially. We had our trusted followers and this was slowly growing. However, we were seen by many locals as 'that expensive organic store', and not for those on low wages with children to feed. The reality of organic food is it's not cheap, nor should it ever be. It cannot be produced ethically and sustainably without having a significant price premium compared with chemically dependent food produced on an industrial scale for which the taxpayer foots the bill for the destruction and havoc caused by its means

The Bristol Proving House,
St Werburghs, 2001

of production. This is a conundrum that haunts the organic movement to this day. I have been interviewed by the press many times, but never without being questioned about organic food being too expensive for many.

Organic food is generally the right price. Non-organic food is generally the wrong price. Non-organic food is based around a model of abusive exploitation and plunder that has no interest in paying for the true cost of the mess it makes both environmentally and also in terms of human health. Organic food is based around a model of generating the health of the soil, plants, animals and humankind. All costs are up front.

With large-scale chemical vegetable and fruit production around the world, prices have been driven down and down, in some cases this means there are migrants labouring like slaves, living in appalling conditions, all to ensure our peppers or apricots don't cost too much in the supermarkets. On top of the exploitation of the people involved, this growing system is mining the soil until it is totally inert and dead. The cost to biodiversity and soil health is enormous. Lastly there is the cost to our health. Produce from farms like these tend to have low nutrient values and this impacts on its health benefits, which in turn leads to ill health.

Adding all of these external costs back into the cost of food production, you find it is far from cheap. Cheap food is in fact expensive. Good food is the right price. The Sustainable Food Trust has done great work around this. See the resources page for information about 'true cost accounting'. Ⓡ

155

Box schemes

In the beginning, a veg box was much more than a box of vegetables. It was a way to make the livelihoods of small-scale organic growers actually possible. It was not only about getting organic produce to market, but about a direct relationship between people and where their food comes from. It was about reducing food miles, decentralising the market, and bringing about wider social and economic change. The best vegetable box schemes are still all about this.

The first scheme I was aware of was started by Guy Watson (Riverford Organics) in 1987. Then came Tim and Jan Deane of Northwood Farm in 1991, whose scheme became a model used throughout the UK and Europe. These types of schemes were known as Community Supported Agriculture or CSAs.

As a route to market, a box scheme remains important to producers to this day. However, our approach has altered as the general public's expectations have shifted to demanding greater convenience, a say in what goes into their boxes and when they get their delivery. In other words, many producers have had to move away from the true CSA model to one that is more about customer satisfaction and retention. The newer bigger players in the delivery market such as Ocado, Amazon and the supermarkets have given us ever more 'convenience' and ever more detachment from the heart and soul of our food. These companies make little or no direct profit out of delivering fresh food. They do it to gain market share and data access.

Fresh and abundant vegetables,
direct from the producer

How you can help your local producers

Have a box of delicious fresh vegetables delivered every week by a producer-led scheme, preferably very local that supports your local economy and often many social projects. Or go to a local independent store to buy similar products often from the same growers. Each pound you spend with a local producer-led box scheme will strengthen your local economy and support more jobs than any of the larger business box schemes.

Bordeaux Quay

In 2004 my brother Barny opened Bordeaux Quay. This was a huge, cavernous place at the end of a run of waterside warehouses at the heart of Bristol's harbour. It was a beautifully redesigned venue, fitted out to be an inspirational fine dining restaurant upstairs and bistro downstairs with a fabulous cookery school at the back.

Barny applied his organic principles and a love and depth of understanding of food to this venture and Bordeaux Quay became nationally recognised. He made history for the scale of what was delivered through the back door from some great farmers and suppliers and lovingly turned into delicious dishes. The customers were treated to great hospitality and culinary delight.

It was a seriously tough operation to manage and get right. Particularly at that time, it wasn't easy to run a restaurant in this way, with such sensitivity to the source of the food. Barny's vision showed the way in respect of food quality, provenance and environmental impact. When the time came to move on, Barny continued his brilliant cookery school project started at Bordeaux Quay - teaching children and adults about food from the soil up. His ability to engage with all who entered the school left them inspired and enriched. This teaching has now become the centre of Barny's life's work. See page 39 for more about him.

The second Better Food shop

The Whiteladies Road store

In 2011, Better Food was on the move again and we were ready to open another store that fostered community along with a greater understanding of our food and where it comes from. We chose Whiteladies Road, Clifton, a mere 1.5 miles from our St Werburghs store. Having gutted the site and rebuilt it as a food hall, we opened in Nov 2011.

Sheer optimism had led me to believe that this project would be an easy one. Yet, despite a good team, it took us a while to crack Whiteladies Road. While it was true that we had a fair few known customers who along with many other locals formed a small customer base, we knew we had to find a lot more and that proved to be a challenge. I never saw Better Food as being about us as a business. For me it was always about working in a better way with better food for all. We had to learn fast what our new customers wanted and we had to work hard just to keep the store open and economically viable.

Luckily, our St Werburghs store was profitable enough to support the WLR store losses and as time went on it did become the community store I envisioned. To create true community I recognise now that you have to give it time to blossom.

The Whiteladies Road store has for many years now been a community store much loved by many. It has a very different feel to St Werburghs and has dished up some fabulous delights from its kitchen. Every so often someone comes along in the life of a business and adds a unique part. At Whiteladies Road it was Lou that did this with deli food. Lou proved to be a brilliant creative cook, able to think on her feet and utilise anything she had available. Fizzing with high tempo energy, Lou mixed her significant cooking talents with a passion for sharing with customers. To add to this Lou knew a lot about nutrition and so often customers left not only with warm-hearted food, but a mini nutrition class too.

Waste not, want not

As well as being a warm welcoming place to eat, drink, talk and rest, the Better Food ethos in catering is to waste nothing. The first café I opened was in part a way of using what would go to waste, such as short-date products and bendy vegetables. This is important both ethically and economically. Waste in supermarkets is at times scandalous, and this alternative approach that we have been following for many years at Better Food has helped us not only reduce waste but also to benefit financially. Using 100% organic vegetables is a rare thing in catering because of the increased costs. Being able to use so-called waste to reduce the ingredient costs of our soups and stews brings us a little closer to competitors using non-organic vegetables. The soups created in our cafés are often based around farm gluts, often resulting in a terrific celebration of the season.

Farinata

(kindly provided by Lou Marchionne)

This recipe should make two or three farinata.

Ingredients

250 g chickpea flour (or gram or besan flour)
1 teaspoon each of sea salt and black pepper
(or less depending on your taste)
50–75 ml good extra virgin olive oil
25 g or about 4 sprigs of rosemary, leaves only
and chopped into the batter. Save some leaves
to top the farinata – they make it look pretty!
(Or in the summer you could make it with basil.)
400 ml sparkling water
2 tablespoons olive oil for the frying pan

Method

Preheat the oven to 200 deg C.

Put the chickpea flour into a bowl with the
sea salt and black pepper. (Farinata needs
seasoning well or it will taste bland.) Make a
well in the centre, pour in the extra virgin olive
oil and then whisk in the water. Then add the
chopped herbs.

Mix until you have a smooth batter, then set
aside to rest for as long as you can, at least
30 minutes. I have started making mine the
day before I want it and leaving it overnight.
It starts to ferment which gives it more life
and helps it rise in the pan, making it more
like bread and less like a pancake. This batter
needs the time to soften and to bind.

When I used to make this every day at the
Better Food deli I used to treat the batter a
little like a sourdough. I would always make
enough batter to leave some for topping up the
next day. The results were a lovely, well risen,
bread-like farinata, served warm with soups,
stews or salads. Customers would come in and
request it. Some used to buy a whole one to
take home.

When the batter has rested, place a large non-
stick frying pan over a medium heat. When hot,
add 1 to 2 tablespoons of olive oil and swirl
in the pan to coat the base of the pan evenly.
Gently ladle or pour the batter into the pan. It
should sizzle. Then sprinkle a few more of the
rosemary leaves or chopped basil on top and
cook on the stove for about 5 minutes.

When the farinata lifts easily from the pan
using a heatproof spatula, turn it over to cook
on the other side. This will only take a few
minutes.

(Alternatively, if the pan is ovenproof, put it
on the middle shelf of a hot oven and bake it
without turning for about 15 minutes until it is
cooked through, is golden brown and will easily
lift away from the pan. Or you could try putting
it under a medium to hot grill.)

When cooked, slide the farinata onto a plate
or a board large enough to then slice it, drizzle
with a little more oil if you would like.

After turning it, you could also top it with
cheese or caramelised onions or both.

It is at its best when served warm with
a soup, a dip, a salad, antipasti or a stew.

Enjoy!

Transforming the food offering of an iconic Bristol arts centre

In 2012 I was asked by my friend Nelisha Wickremasinghe to talk with Dick Penny, CEO of the Watershed about their catering offer. Nelisha felt that my experience gave me a unique qualification to help them. The Watershed, is known to almost everyone in Bristol as a beacon of film culture and creative technology. Its catering enterprise back at that time was a little sad, with rather ordinary food.

I set about working with them to bring about a big change in approach. 'Plot to plate' would be the new theme with a real commitment to local and organic food. For such an important local community-orientated media organisation and business to be prepared to work in this way was a wonderful thing for Bristol. I hunted down a chef, Oliver Pratt, who

I felt could take it on. First, I interviewed Oli, then I took him to our field below Barley Wood Walled Gardens to explore soil matters and explain the core of what we were trying to do. I asked him to pick some ingredients and cook me a meal, which he did with flair and care. He had proved to me that he was passionate, caring and understood the needs of the business.

With some mentoring and support, Oli triumphed at the Watershed café. He made it work, shifting old habits into a new approach, all the time paying attention to margins and staffing costs. I am grateful for Dick's openminded approach and to Oli's passion to take it forward. Many years on, Watershed café is still delivering a little of that ethos. Public places like this can be game changers in people's habits around food as they hold the power to normalise what is good and change people's food behaviour. Let's celebrate the places like this that go the extra mile in food ethics!

Why not ask your favourite local media or arts place to adopt a local and organic food policy?

Watershed Café

Losing ethical brands to international corporates

At Better Food, we work to only stock ethical products in our stores, yet it is not always easy to make a call on what to stock and what to drop. Our customers have been great at keeping us on our toes. There are several fantastic brands that were pioneers in the ethical and organic world, driven by the passion of their founders. 'Rachel's Dairy', 'Green & Blacks', 'Ecover', 'Pukka Herbs', to name a few, are now all owned by international food conglomerates. We have dropped all except Pukka which was sold to Unilever in 2017.

In 1999 Rachel's Dairy were bought by Horizon a US dairy company who were bought out by others and now Nestlé own 40% of the company.

In 2005 Green and Blacks were sold to Cadbury and this was closely followed by Cadbury being sold to Kraft. This led us to drop them as a supplier because we were not convinced that Cadbury shared our ethics or had a genuine interest in organic. Although the brand had a strong following, we made this decision and never looked back, in part because there were new organic brands coming on the market with some superb innovative ways to entice us to eat fabulous flavours and styles of chocolate.

At a trade show in the late 1980s in Brighton, I talked with Ecover who told me they had no intention of ever supplying the supermarkets. However, they did go on to do so and later still they were bought by Group4 who have interests in the arms trade. So with time, we eventually got rid of the last of their products from our shelves. There are some great alternatives so it wasn't a difficult decision to make.

Celebrating local brands and produce

Sometimes these big companies, such as Kraft, Nestlé, Group4, and Unilever water down the environmental and ethical standards of the founders of these smaller businesses they take over. Where the original owners may have cared deeply about fair trade, the people in their supply chain, or the integrity of their ingredients, these global conglomerates, beholden first and foremost to lining the pockets of their shareholders are now much more focused on offering strong financial returns. This model is not only damaging the health of people and our planet, it is creating a massive blight on our financial system as a whole.

Our relationship with Pukka has continued. I know and love Tim and Seb who founded Pukka and what they stand for. They care deeply about people and the planet and have sold to Unilever. I recognised that Unilever are certainly doing some good ethical work in the world. In fact, I believe that Unilever would like to change the face of the corporate world and I wish them well in facing down the corporate shareholder

Happy shoppers in St Werburghs community store

power. When any large corporate gets hold of an independent brand built on ethics and love, it is difficult for that smaller business to retain all of its values. I believe it is inevitable it will lose its roots and roots are critical to the life of any healthy tree.

One approach might be to lobby companies such as Unilever to drop unethical brands and really up their game in championing sustainable and organic products. Global food companies generally do not serve humanity well and I suspect it's time to begin to dismantle these structures. Of course, this would challenge the whole notion of international brands and could potentially lose thousands of brands we love. However, it would do enormous amounts for local food economies, helping more local independents to thrive and benefit. In a matter of a

Small companies are fuelled by a passion to make their products a success

decade we would see a huge increase in the diversity of food offerings. Small companies generally don't run their businesses by spreadsheets, but are fuelled by a passion to make their products a success. Change of this magnitude may only come because the world has been forced into it due to the climate emergency. So long as it's easy to move goods across this globe we will go on consuming them.

At Better Food we have been blessed with great people working for us who, alongside our customers, have challenged and continue to challenge what we do. All this helps keep us from being too fixed and remain focused on what is best for all. We seem to attract people who are thinking about the world and want to make a difference. I am delighted to say this has included many budding entrepreneurs over the years. Lately we have brought in new product lines that were developed by people in our own team.

Mike Duckworth gradually wound down his hours working at Better Food over two years as he built his own brand of vegan nut butters suitable for those with peanut allergies. He now has his own business, Nutcessity, distributing all around the country.

Bea Steinhoerster made wonderful cherry stone heat bags called Warmpillow to help with aches and stiffness.

Grzegorz Macalla is still with us and makes delectable vegan chocolates as a part-time business to help supplement his family income and because he loves it.

All of these showed and promoted their products in Better Food with pride and a great story. Over the decades, many have passed through and gone on to grow their own enterprises.

The crowds fund a new store

In 2015, the team decided that we were ready to look at opening a new store. I wanted this store to be a more overt flagship for non-supermarket shopping, for a celebration of strong ethics, of independent retail and its suppliers. We found a site that really caught our imagination. There were some hoardings around a big site by the old Bristol Gaol, and an old coal yard down behind Bristol's industrial museum, the MShed. The billboards were advertising what was being developed on the site and part of that was for independent retailers to take the business units below the flats.

I contacted Stuart Hatton from the developers, Umberslade. Stuart and I met and I immediately got excited by Stuart's vison that all units be taken by independent businesses, a rare thing in new developments as most developers are super risk averse and tend to go for the same old chains.

The new site is close to the harbour waterfront and it has a growing number of flats close by. Excitingly for us, it was a new build and the architecture was really strong. The idea of having a blank canvas inside the store was one I relished. A chance to design and fit out from the concrete floor up. My days of begging, borrowing and using credit cards to finance growth were over. This time we looked into crowdfunding. With a good brand reputation and track record we felt we had a great opportunity. After talks with two crowdfunder platform operators we were a bit aghast at the interest rates they felt we would need to offer backers – between 11% and 12.5%. This was not viable for us. I also knew Jamie Hartzell from Ethex, an ethical financial platform that could offer crowdfund services partnering up with the investment arm of Triodos Bank, who I had started banking with back in the 1990s. They were able to offer access to a mini-bond, and at a much lower interest rate of 7%. While this still seemed a bit high, I understood the investor risk element. If we failed, they lost their money. Time was short and we were so close to signing the deal with Umberslade we decided to take the plunge.

The Triodos investment arm got into gear and with flair and efficiency got the mini-bond ready to launch in record time. This was sent out to both the Triodos and Ethex dedicated investor lists of people. We had to raise £350k in 30 days. Never having done this, we thought it would be a lot of work and need a great deal of social media publicity and promotion to try and get customers and others to take a slice. You can imagine our delight when we logged in on day one to see that investors had already started to pledge good amounts, and as the days went on we were all smiles. By day 10 we were £70k oversubscribed. Wow! This was quite something and was a huge affirmation of us as a company and brand as well as our store plans.

I knew I wanted this store to have strong roots to anchor its fast-moving trade of local residents on their way to work. I had a vision of solid English oak flooring with recycled pallet board edging. We used a local blacksmith to make legs for all our café tables designed with the harbour cranes in mind. My brother Luke made beautiful English oak table tops. With every step we thought about the ethics and the environmental impact of what we were doing.

Better food retailing

Food retail is a crazy business. It's very tight on margins and it moves incredibly fast. If we don't manage wage targets, we can lose money. If we don't nail sales margins we can lose money. If we don't keep close control over every purchase and every mini-project then we can lose money. In other words, to succeed in food retail you have to be sharp and attentive all the time. On top of all this there is this very strange beast called the market. It's fickle. The season, the media, the weather, the country's governance, and even the moon and the universe. It's a bit like getting up in the morning, sometimes you wake up bright and full of the joys of spring. Other days, for no reason, you just feel a bit lacking in vim and vigour. These things affect how you are with family, colleagues and of course when and how you shop and eat.

There is so much to celebrate about being in a business with purpose

Of course, it would be easier for retailers if people were predictable. Yet days when you sell out of bread, or sell 20% less bread, are part of what we work with daily. In some ways, it is to be celebrated, because we have to think about waste, about not having enough, and about how we take convenience for granted.

It is without doubt easier to make a loss on turnover than it is to make a profit. The market would suggest that we should look for 4% or more net profit. We have never even approached this, but we do need to make at least 1.5% to be secure. We aspire to 3%. This would enable us to reinvest in the business and return even more to benefit social projects.

Retailing with ethics, caring about people and having a commitment to a better world, was always going to be harder than the mainstream 'no questions asked' approach. Yet, if there is one thing I know, it's all worth it. There is so much to celebrate about being in a business with purpose, knowing that thousands of people feel fulfilled shopping for and eating great food while directly impacting on soil health, the wellbeing of good farmers and the healing of our shared earth.

Outdoor displays at a Better Food store

A word about oak

When you walk into the Wapping Wharf store, you will notice the beautiful oak floors. I believe, beyond what you see, that oak feeds the soul. It feels well earthed and alive. It adds a little bit of wellbeing to the shopping experience that would not be there if we had used soulless engineered boards. This fast-paced retail site has around 7000 commuters crossing the bridge just next to us daily. It's my belief that the oak helps people slow down - just a little. The oak tree is very powerful and has blessed our store with soul.

The Oak

I Oak stand hard and strong
I am here but 300 years
Come, Bend forth my bough
Take a sprig and share
Break the back of a limb
Or Saw me clean down
I will not flinch, but yield to the next
Build a home with my trunk
Long enduring and beautiful it will be
Warm your new home
With my limbs and remember
Now is your time
Plant the acorns of my kin
And in 300 years they will surely
be there to yield to the next

Ped Asgarian
Environmental activist

Ped originally studied environmental sciences at University, but spent the next decade mixing travelling with the operational and commercial management of small to medium sized business in the food retail sector. Ped spent six years as managing director of The Community Farm - a CSA and social enterprise working to revolutionise and innovate the food system for the betterment of people and the planet. He is a founding member and sits on the board of Bristol Food Producers, an organisation aiming to upscale local food production and distribution.

Writing this in the midst of the Covid-19 pandemic that is sweeping the globe allows for interesting reflections on business models and the impacts they have had, are having and may continue to have in the years to come. We have built a capitalist society that is founded on increasing profits under the false promise of a better life for all. Work hard and you will climb ladders; the creation of an ambition to be rich and prosperous to achieve social status at the cost of anything. These are principles which are fed to us from a young age. This drive has caused ever increasing divides between the rich and poor, and larger numbers of people living below the breadline every year. Our modern society may be praised as the result of progression achieved through capitalism (longer life expectancy, greater medical advancements, and so on), but I think you have to judge a society in the context of what it could achieve with the knowledge and technology it has at its disposal. We have the power to achieve positive change together, addressing global issues such as food insecurity, inequality, crippling sovereign debts and access to clean water - but we do not.

Good business should be at the heart of how we address these issues, guiding us through example and best practice. We must move away from the destructive drive of profit for shareholders being the primary aim for business, and place a stronger emphasis on people and the planet before all else. Empathy and care for all living things needs to be adopted, and business practices changed to benefit communities and the local environment. The notion that 50% of global wealth is held by 1% of the population cannot persist any longer. I am not saying that capitalism is wrong. Yet the state of our planet has exposed the fact that the version of capitalism we have carved out is no longer fit for purpose. Change will not be easy, and we need to implement systemic change that will challenge many of our belief systems never previously questioned. You can't help but feel that right now is the perfect opportunity to do so. I want to be able to talk proudly of the change we made to the next generation, not hide in shame because we allowed humanity and this planet to suffer.

Green eggs and ham

A simple and delicious breakfast that works all year round

Poached eggs
Ham
Bread (good quality granary, rye or sourdough)
King oyster mushroom
Cherry tomatoes - halved

For the pesto

Spinach/chard/beet leaf
Wild garlic or basil
Olive oil
Pine nuts
Garlic clove
Parmesan cheese
Salt and pepper for seasoning

It goes without saying... ingredients should be sourced locally, seasonally and ethically.

Method

Make your pesto first. Toast the pine nuts and then mix them with your chosen green and the garlic or basil in a blender. Add a couple of tablespoons olive oil and some shavings of parmesan and give a final whizz. Remove from the blender and season to taste. I like my pesto to still have a crunch from the parmesan and pine nuts so I don't blend too much.

Slice the king oyster mushroom lengthways and cook on a griddle with your bread. Give both a splash of oil before you cook them.

Boil some water and add it to a pan with a generous splash of white wine vinegar and salt. When it's boiling gently, crack the eggs straight in. Cook for 2½ minutes and then allow to sit off the heat for a further 30 seconds before removing the eggs onto a paper towel to dry off.

Assemble your breakfast. Place the bread on your plate and generously apply the pesto, add the ham next followed by the eggs. Garnish with the mushroom and cherry tomatoes and finish by seasoning with salt and pepper.

Resources
Better business

Organisations for better business

Bio Leadership is an important part of future organisational and business ways of working.
https://bio-leadership.org

BCorps
Certified BCorps are a new kind of business that balances purpose and profit. They are legally required to consider the impact of their decisions on their workers, customers, suppliers, community, and the environment. This is a community of leaders, driving a global movement of people using businesses as a force for good.
https://bcorporation.uk

Ethex
Ethex is a small not-for-profit organisation based in Oxford, UK with the aim of creating a marketplace for positive investments.
https://www.ethex.org.uk/

Triodos Bank
The bank's mission is to help create a society that protects and promotes quality of life and human dignity for all.
https://www.triodos.co.uk

Books

Duncan, Sarah (2019) *The Ethical Business Book: 50 ways you can help protect people, the planet and profits*, Lid Publishing.

Hargreaves, Paul (2019) *Forces for Good: Creating a better world through purpose-driven businesses*, SRA Books.

Pretty, Jules (2002) *Agri-culture: Reconnecting people*, land and nature, Routledge

Reed, Matthew (2010) *Rebels for the Soil: The rise of the global organic food and farming movement*, Earthscan

Watson, Guy (2008) *Riverford Farm Cook Book: Tales from the fields, recipes from the kitchen*, Fourth Estate

Articles, blogs, web

McGowan, Natasha (updated 2019) 'What is an ethical business?', Startups, https://startups.co.uk/what-is-an-ethical-business/ (accessed 11 June 2020)

Nature and More, 'What is true cost accounting?', https://www.natureandmore.com/en/true-cost-of-food/what-is-true-cost-accounting (accessed 11 June 2020)

School for Social Entrepreneurs, 'What funding is available for social entrepreneurs?', https://www.the-sse.org/resources/starting/what-funding-is-available-for-social-entrepreneurs/ (accessed 11 June 2020)

Soil Association, 'Box Schemes are a really easy way to choose organic', https://www.soilassociation.org/organic-living/buy-organic/find-an-organic-box-scheme/ (accessed 11 June 2020)

Sustainable Food Trust, 'True cost accounting', https://sustainablefoodtrust.org/key-issues/true-cost-accounting/ (accessed 11 June 2020)

Van Bussel, Kieran (2018), 'What is the best structure for a social enterprise?', Michelmores, https://www.michelmores.com/news-views/news/what-best-structure-social-enterprise (accessed 11 June 2020)

Better future

Pulling together today to create a better tomorrow

So where do we go from here? As I write, in the midst of the Covid-19 pandemic, I am aware that in recent months for many there has been a rise in connection to community, to nature and to our food. It is these elements of life on earth that support us. We have a chance, right now, to choose a world with more compassion and to nurture what it really means to be human.

Sorting out our future is, of course, complex. If we do begin to get CO_2 levels down to something manageable, this is just the start. If we come to the realisation that part of that work involves rebuilding biodiversity this is just one more step. The biggest challenge is to do all this while truly understanding that, above all, we need to look after each other - in our families, in our schools, in our communities, in our country and across cultures.

So, while we may have no idea what tomorrow will bring, yet with our young people at the vanguard of developing new pathways then maybe, just maybe, what unfolds in our world will be more hopeful. Maybe we can make a seismic shift in how we organise ourselves on this incredible planet that we share with the rest of nature.

We have an opportunity at this juncture in human development to do things differently. To farm as if nature were our teacher, to attend to the human spirit and our connectedness to the mystery that surrounds us, to nurture community as the foundation of our ability to express ourselves fully, and to foster humility as a daily act of love.

Phil talked to...
Caroline Lucas

Caroline is the Green Party MP for Brighton Pavilion. She was an MEP for 10 years, before being elected as the Green Party's first MP in 2010.

Phil: Tell me what's important to you about our future on Mother Earth.

Caroline: Human wellbeing depends most fundamentally on healthy ecosystems and a liveable climate, not economic growth. We've known this for ages, but we still run our economies as if our environment was simply a resource to exploit – whether that's for food production or as a dumping ground for pollution and waste. We urgently need a new relationship with nature – and with each other too. Under the current economic system, it's not just wildlife and biodiversity that are suffering; inequality and poverty are widespread too.

Caroline: This is about political choices. We can choose to have a better economy that's based on care and compassion – for each other and for the natural world. And we can choose to put cooperation over competition as the powerful force for progress that will get us there.

Phil: Do you have any suggestions for people as to how they can do/act/work to make change in the world?

Caroline: Food is a perfect place to start. What we eat, how our food is grown, and where we buy it from are ways to make a positive difference to the climate and nature emergency every day. Such choices have major implications for animal protection, our health and the local economy too. However, not everyone can access adequate, healthy, sustainably produced food. Only a fraction of UK farmland is organic. The number of people relying on food banks is a national scandal.

That's why I think it's important for us to act as food citizens – not just as consumers. That might include improving workplace food sourcing, getting involved in local growing projects, lobbying local councillors, or writing to parliamentarians to demand new laws to cut pesticide use, improve animal welfare or boost organic farming. Just as public health cannot be left to the market, neither can food.

Phil: What do our leaders and governors need to do most to help make change?

Caroline: We should prioritise putting the Right to Food into law, and embarking on a transition to agroecological farming as the norm. Agroecology is all about producing food in harmony with nature, and with full consideration of social aspects. Fairer wages and more localised supply chains are essential too. There are already many practical examples of what a better food future would look like: from 'rebel supermarkets' like HISBE in Brighton, to urban and peri-urban food growing, community supported agriculture and organic farming. Political leaders need to put in place the policies to scale this up.

Fundamentally, we need a different economic system to prioritise what matters the most. We need an economy that is designed to enhance human and environmental health and wellbeing as a top priority, rather than seeking to infinitely increase consumption and growth on a finite planet.

Soda bread with beetroot and caraway

(based on a recipe by Anna Jones)

Makes I large loaf

Ingredients

300 g grated beetroot
100 ml plain yoghurt
150 g strong wholewheat flour
250 g white spelt flour
1 teaspoon roasted fennel seeds
2 teaspoon roasted caraway seeds
1 teaspoon sea salt
2 teaspoon bicarbonate of soda
A pinch ground black pepper

Method

Preheat the oven to 220 deg C.

Cook the beetroot in a few tablespoons of water until soft. Drain but keep any excess water.

Put all the flour, 1 teaspoon of caraway, all the fennel seeds, salt, bicarbonate of soda and pepper into a large bowl and mix well.

Pour the beetroot and the yoghurt into the flour mix and stir with a fork, add enough beetroot water to get a doughy consistency, then use your hands to bring the lot into a rough ball without any kneading.

Sprinkle flour onto a baking sheet and put your mix onto this. Scatter your other teaspoon of caraway seeds on top.

Cut a deep (a good 2.5 cm) cross into the top of the loaf and bake for about 40 minutes, until well risen and brown. It's cooked when you get a hollow sound on tapping the bottom of the loaf. Leave to cool on a rack.

This goes brilliantly with Irish butter and a borscht soup.

A better future for nature

Our future is so inextricably linked to us connecting at a deep level with nature. Nature is our great healer and teacher. Nowhere have I felt this more than through working with 8 Shields, the global movement that connects us with nature in a vital way. It utilises a finely tuned, tried and tested mentoring model that has proved to create healthy and vibrant leaders and nature-based intergenerational mentoring communities all around the world. (See Better nature, page 14 for an interview with Jon Young, founder of 8 Shields.)

Ever since I was 17 I have immersed myself in nature. It was easy to be close to it in the Galloway Hills. In the five years I spent in Scotland, I developed a deep love of the land and soil, and its ability to support incredible amounts of wildlife. It was common to see peewits, cuckoos and, on rare occasions, a pine marten. I farmed our 17 acres of land organically and all was well.

After 45 years of my own immersion in organic food and farming, it's a tragedy to be aware that we have lost so much of our precious wildlife. We razed our hedges, we decided monocrops of grass with a massive input of chemical fertilisers was the way forward. We ploughed our lands to the edge of every boundary and poured chemicals onto every crop. We made our cows into milk machines that halved their life expectancy, then went still further and put them in huge barns all year. We damaged every aspect of agriculture in just a few generations, leaving our food often sanitised and soulless.

Now, we are just starting to wake up to the catastrophic consequences of all of this to our wildlife, to our climate, and to our health and wellbeing. The human disconnection from nature is at last being noticed and we are learning to reconnect.

And so we arrive at the most critical point in human history. We are living with climate anxiety as a very real phenomenon, felt by most of civilisation. Our very species is at stake. The planet would not even notice if we were to fade out. It will continue to react, rebalance and thrive. Our future is not about saving the planet, it is about acting as if the Earth matters. After all, it is the Earth that is our true ancestor. Before humans were animals. Before animals were sea creatures and before this, plants and before this … well it was simply the planet. Human life has never been necessary for planetary life to thrive.

It is only humanity that can save itself from extinction.

It is our time to get out there and pull our human destructive force back from the brink, to learn to live within the rules of the natural world. Nature is miraculous in its ability to recover fast. Given the chance and the right support it will heal our lands and our forests, re-stock the earth with the diverse wildlife we have lost in such a short space of time. During the lockdown caused by the Covid-19 pandemic human domination has visibly edged back. The birdsong is louder, and previously no-go areas are suddenly available to wildlife. If we can allow this to happen then the positive impact on carbon sequestration and on biodiversity will be massive, the impact on communities will be rich and positive and humanity will have lots to be grateful for and to celebrate.

Our future is about acting as if the Earth matters

Cooking and eating together deserves our commitment as a building block of good culture

A better future for cooking and eating

Our high streets were originally designed as places to provide goods and services to local communities, a marketplace and a meeting place for traders and people. When weekly markets eventually became daily and permanent, we called them shops. These days our high streets have changed beyond recognition. They have little to do with needs in any sense of the word and a great deal to do with global brands vying for our attention and our money. We now see that this model is failing as it collapses in the face of Covid-19.

When approaching Whiteladies Road in Bristol in my little electric car I often look up and notice the Edwardian frontages. There is one particularly handsome old sign for the Redland Fish Supply Company painted onto the Bath stone high up on the walls. However, Whiteladies has not been a happy shopping street for a significant number of years. There are around 12 or so furniture, kitchen and sofa shops, which are now starting to close down. Other trades are missing. The DIY store closed after only two years, there are no clothes shops left, no book shops, no bakery. Yet it is possible that all traders could do well if they opened up on this street providing a full range of goods and services at a local level.

Having the critical mass is what makes a shopping street work. On the other side of town, there is the very different Gloucester Road. This is a hive of independents retailers - a hardworking, creative bunch determined to keep this street alive and serving a large local population with most of what they need and want. Interestingly the supermarkets have in the past 10 years or so made it more likely that independent food stores can thrive on the highstreets. When they chose to focus more on convenience stores and less on large out of town malls, they brought the shopper back to the high street. Now is the time to open food stores close to these supermarket convenience stores where they can often thrive. The support for localism is growing in a way I have not seen in my trading life and this offers us hope that we can take back our high streets in the name of better food and stronger, safer communities.

We almost all have to shop before we cook and eat, and when we shop in streets full of independents, it makes us feel good in comparison to the supermarket experience. Covid-19 brought millions of families back to their kitchens and to sharing the experience of cooking and eating together. During the lockdown brought about by the pandemic, more time has been spent together around food than for the past 50 years or more, be that baking bread or simply cooking our meals from scratch. On top of this we've re-learned how to use what's been available while the choice in shops has been limited. For many of us this opportunity arose because we had more time on our hands. We can reflect on what this time has offered us and realise once more that cooking and eating together is fundamental to being human and it deserves our commitment as a building block of good culture.

A better future for farming and growing

Producing food for people to eat while being custodians of healthy soils, a diverse wildlife habitat and enhancing the landscape for all to access and connect with.

This is what our farmers and growers can do if we ask them to.

For the sake of all our futures we would do well to celebrate and cherish any food producers that live up to these ideals and encourage all others to join this vital approach to feeding the world. There is a new urgency to design appropriate tools to help us cultivate and tend our soils and plants. Many people are rejecting the route towards more automation and robotics and trusting that our hands are important to use in food production. It is so much better to use simple tools that aid our hands rather than working to replace them entirely.

Growing food can and perhaps needs to be an effort based in the community. When we, the public, see what it really takes to produce food sustainably our attitudes change. Having been in some way involved in farming and growing, we can celebrate the joy of being nourished fully, body and soul, by delicious, health-giving food and truly appreciate our farmers and growers work for humanities wellbeing.

66
With strong connection to farming we can better appreciate our food

Some children are now being offered access to projects such as city farms, community growing projects and school allotments that teach them about food and farming in a more caring way. And we can do so much more in our schools and universities to bring food to the fore in education. With strong connection to farming we can better appreciate our food and what it takes to produce it with compassion for our animals, our soils and for biodiversity. It's time to build on the thousands of amazing projects as a model for the future for all young people.

Growing Communities,
Hackney, London

A better future for community

Strong communities of the future are the same in essence as good communities of the past. I think some additions for a better future are vital.

'Humankind has not woven the web of life. We are but one thread within it. Whatever we do to the web, we do to ourselves. All things are bound together. All things connect...' (Chief Seattle, 1854)

When I think about the world's future I oscillate between being filled with anxiety about the end of humankind as we know it and feeling hopeful and inspired by human endeavour and creativity. The truth is we can't fully know what's around the corner and so we can only to do our best to live today well. The Transition Movement have set off so many good conversations and practical actions to build resilience for the future. And now we have the fast growing XR movement taking our governments to task in a way that cannot be ignored. It's inspiring a global awakening, not just to our climate issues, but to how we live together on our precious planet. This movement is asking us to explore our hearts and truly attempt to connect with all we see and feel. ®

We are experimenting constantly. New ways are being explored for diverse groups to work together and models are being created that no longer see the patriarchal system as relevant to our future health and wellbeing. We are discovering alternative ways to protect, ways to connect more fully, ways to hold meetings that value all contributions equally, and of course ways to celebrate the value of groups and communities. There is a small group called Blue Moon in the US who use the term 'radical hospitality'. This group are passionate about getting things done with love and offering space to grow as humans within a framework of mutuality. Radical hospitality is commonly associated with religious groups, but actually it's simply an approach to living that is full of love and kindness, where giving freely with love for the sake of life on earth changes lives. ®

Some of our more recent ancestors valued elders in their society and culture. These cultures were often deeply connected to earth and the cosmos. These elders, whether spiritual or social, were critical to peace, to communing with all around them. Our culture today has increasingly disconnected itself from elders, causing imbalance and room for greed and power to take hold. Today, the need for eldering and mentoring in our culture is re-entering our collective consciousness. Those who have gone before offer us checks and balances, they hold the edges of our culture, ensuring it does not stray into the long grass where the snakes hide. We do well to hold them close.

Let our young radical people take centre stage in designing community fit for our future, but listening carefully to the wisdom of elders, and to sit and to listen to what the Earth has to say.

We can only do our best to live today well

A better future for business

For thousands of years business has largely been divided into two groups – those focused on maximum profit and exploitation of resources, and those devoted to serving local communities. There is no room left in our world for those pursuing maximum profit and exploitation of resources. To dismantle this requires a huge leap for humankind as we all use it, rely on it and depend on it to some extent.

New options in business are continually being created by forward thinking people, like the co-ops of old, the BCorps of new, community interest companies, community benefit societies along with the adoption of non-hierarchical flat organisational structures where diversity and new ways in leadership such as Bio Leadership, which uses nature as its guide. They all serve to challenge the status quo of the business world and offer new and evolving toolkits. All pay more attention to the part business must play in wider society, understanding that business impacts enormously on culture and community cohesion.

There is no room left in our world for those pursuing maximum profit and exploitation of resources

Over the past few years I have been inspired and energised to look at how we might bring some new approaches to how we work in Better Food. We can all become vehicles for 'village building', helping to foster more connected communities where all people really count and where particular attention is paid to nature since it holds all our needs. Organisations are communities and many of them are outward looking. They can be a great force for connection with nature as well as for wider societal change.

Better Food shops for the future

Back in 2016, we witnessed the success and energy created from the opening of our third store in terms of support from both investors and customers. This confirmed my intuition that Better Food is loved and is a good thing for all communities. Our stores do not only provide healthy food for sustenance, they also provide a connection from soil-to-farmer-to-fork. In addition to that 'connection' experience that people thirst for we give our customers choices that they can't get at the supermarkets. And each year, we are seeing our customer base grow as a result. This growth helps build sustainable demand for organic produce, which is essential to give farmers confidence and opportunity to grow more organic produce. In turn, if we grow more organic, we need more organic land. And, the more organic land we have the healthier our soils and carbon capture - an amazing virtuous circle for a better world.

It occurred to me, what if we had more stores like this? Lots more! What would the world look like? For example, if we went on to open 100 stores under a model that was fair and caring of all, we might be

Better Food could help be part of the solution towards a better way and a better world

able to offer a serious alternative to the supermarket experience of shopping and, along with so many others, become a model for a better way. We can't change the world overnight, but Better Food could help be part of the solution towards a better way and a better world. The great thing is that it is within our reach. This is now set out as an ambition for Better Food and we are on the journey. Our plan is to open organic, local, ethical stores all over the UK. Each store would be supported to run as a community hub, with some element of local investment and, of course, local suppliers. Our challenge will always be to ensure that as we grow, new stores are empowered to build their own community and feel supported by a central team, who are themselves answerable to the voice of many communities.

I am touched by how it's grown so far and humbled by all the people that have helped to create this community. I am also energised by the need to keep pushing and keep going for the sole purpose of benefiting more farmers, more employees, more customers and wider communities; all while helping the Earth to protect and repair its precious soils. One hundred stores would make a significant move towards a better world and a legacy I would be proud to have helped bring into being.

Journey 100

Our purpose has always been and always will be to make a better, fairer food community.

With our successful Bristol hub, we are helping thousands of people – employees, customers, suppliers, farmers and other affiliates – every day to make a better world. One fair, earth-friendly transaction at a time at human scale.

We want to increase our positive impact. Exponentially. To do this, we will expand to more communities, in the right way. Positively, ethically and fairly. Our expansion journey has already started and will continue at a manageable, yet accelerating pace. Our aim is 100 stores over the next 20 years.

This is our Journey 100.
Will you join us?

Julie Brown
Growing Communities

Julie Brown is founder and director of Growing Communities in Hackney, London: a social enterprise working to transform food and farming through community-led trade. Julie also founded the Better Food Traders – a national network of ethical businesses selling sustainably grown fresh fruit and veg.

I've been wondering when we were suckered into believing that we could change the world through 'green consumerism'. At Friends of the Earth back in the 1980s this concept made us wary. At the risk of sounding like an Einstein misquote, you can't solve a problem using the same approach that caused the problem in the first place. Moreover, shifting responsibility away from governments and corporations leaves it all (plus the guilt) to individuals and how they spend their money.

Don't get me wrong: the fate of this phenomenal planet does ultimately come down to how much stuff we consume. But most of our impact is embedded in systems providing the basis of society – energy, transport, agriculture, industry, housing, education, healthcare. We can't directly control these through personal consumer choices. (And pitting zerowasters, anti-plastickers, flight-shamers and vegans against each other is as likely to divide and conquer as to achieve effective positive change.)

Unpicking individual versus systemic changes is tricky, but is illustrated in the following reports:

Lund University says the most effective individual changes are:
• Flying less
• Living car-free
• Using green energy
• Eating a mainly plant-based diet

While Project Drawdown ranks the impact of systemic interventions (interestingly, two of the most significant are educating girls and access to affordable contraception):
• Top of the list comes (a bit uninspiringly if I'm honest) refrigeration – replacing HFCs that replaced ozone-depleting CFCs in the 1990s but turned out to have a much higher greenhouse impact
• On-shore wind power (getting more interesting)
• Reducing food waste (now you're talking)
• Moving to plant-rich diets (yay!)

The Better Food Traders operate in the space between individual and systemic. In the early 1990s we realised that we needed radical change in our food system but had no confidence in government legislation, or in food and agriculture industry voluntary reform. So, we set about creating a viable alternative (albeit on a small scale) to aggregate individual choices towards the systemic changes we were seeking.

Over 20-plus years, using the collective buying power of our community, we've shaped the food and farming systems that feed us. We've given organic and agroecological farmers fair and sustainable routes to market; created ethically based supply chains; championed the design-out of waste and pollution and designed in environmental care and community-building, with plant-rich diets at the heart of it all.

For a better food future we need this system to grow and replace the damaging, greedy structure that has brought us to the crisis we're in now.

Spiced veg fritters

This may be the perfect veg box recipe as it's very quick and incredibly adaptable - any veg will do. Just pick your favourite or the best of what's in season. Or whatever you find in your fridge.

Include finely diced onions and garlic for extra flavour. Add pzazz by serving with sweet chilli sauce or a yoghurt raita and a simple salad on the side. Chickpea (gram) flour is gluten-free.

Recommended combinations:
• Courgette, onion and mint
• Grated beetroot and fennel
• Shredded kale with cumin and cayenne
• Grated squash and sage
• Grated carrot and parsnip with cumin and fresh coriander

Makes at least 8 fritters

150 g gram (chickpea) flour
300 g grated or finely chopped veg
Fresh herbs and spices of your choice
Salt and pepper to taste
Oil for frying

In a large bowl mix the flour with water to a smooth double cream consistency. Stir in the vegetables plus any herbs, spices and seasoning. Heat the oil in a frying pan and then put heaped tablespoons of the mixture into the pan.

Fry for about 2 minutes on each side until the fritters are crisp and starting to brown.

Resources
Better future

Organisations for a better future

BCorps
www.bcorporation.uk

Blue Moon Fund
bluemoonfund.org

Extinction Rebellion
rebellion.earth

Project Drawdown - The World's
Leading Resource for Climate
Solutions
www.drawdown.org

Schumacher College
Innovative Learning for
Ecological and Social Change
www.schumachercollege.org.uk

The Bio-Leadership Project
bio-leadership.org

Transition Network
transitionnetwork.org

UK Mindfulness Network
mindfulnesspractice.co.uk

Books

Hechter, Michael (1988) *Principles
of Group Solidarity*, University of
California Press.

Homan, Daniel & Collins Pratt, Lonni
(2007) *Radical Hospitality: Benedict's
way of love*, Wild Goose.

Steel, Carolyn (2020) *Sitopia:
How food can save the world*,
Chatto & Windus.

Articles, blogs, web

Better Food Traders
betterfoodtraders.org

Growing Communities
www.growingcommunities.org/

Nicholas, Kimberley & Wynes, Seth,
'The four lifestyle choices that most
reduce your carbon footprint', Lund
University, https://www.lunduniversity.
lu.se/article/the-four-lifestyle-
choices-that-most-reduce-your-
carbon-footprint (accessed
12 June 2020)

**We need an economy that is
designed to enhance human
and environmental health and
wellbeing as a top priority**

Copyright and credits

Food for Thought: Celebrating the joy of eating well and living better

ISBN 978-1-912300-36-5

Published in 2020 by SRA Books
© Phil Haughton 2020

Design: ollyandtom.co.uk
Commissioned photography: Kirstie Young
Better Food brand photography: Rob Wicks

Unsplash photography: Clem Onojeghuo (page 23), Max Delsid (page 44), Annie Spratt (page 48), Jakob Cotton (page 81), Azimbek Assarov (page 167), Markus Spiske (page 169).